D1231604

JAN 2 9 1992
MAR 2 1 1992
JAN 3 1 1993
FEB 2 7 1993
APR 1 3 1994

Studies in Political Science

Edited by

DR MALCOLM ANDERSON
University of Warwick

4

THE MAKING OF BRITISH
FOREIGN POLICY

THE MAKING OF
BRITISH
FOREIGN POLICY

David Vital
Author of 'The Inequality of States'

London
GEORGE ALLEN AND UNWIN LTD
RUSKIN HOUSE MUSEUM STREET

FIRST PUBLISHED IN 1968

This book is copyright under the Berne Convention.
Apart from any fair dealing for the purposes of private
study, research, criticism or review, as permitted under
the Copyright Act, 1956, no portion may be reproduced
by any process without written permission. Inquiries
should be made to the publishers.

© *George Allen & Unwin Ltd 1968*

SBN 04 327028 x (cased)

04 327029 8 (paper)

ERINDALE
COLLEGE
LIBRARY

PRINTED IN GREAT BRITAIN
in 10 on 11pt Plantin Type
BY WILLMER BROTHERS LIMITED
BIRKENHEAD

CONTENTS

FOREWORD

THIS book is intended to serve a dual purpose. It represents an attempt to set out the processes of foreign policy-making in the United Kingdom; and, at the same time, it is designed to introduce readers to some of the problems of foreign policy analysis. The former purpose is, certainly, the more immediate, but it has seemed to me best to tackle it within an explicit theoretical framework in the hope that a discussion, however limited, of the general theoretical problems involved would serve both to elucidate the account of the specifically British topics and make the approach on which the study as a whole is founded as unambiguous as possible. For it is, of course, quite fruitless to attempt to analyze a complex subject of this kind with all its intricate political, institutional and sociological ramifications except on the basis of some view of what is or is not significant, what does or does not constitute a valid explanation (however the term 'explanation' may be conceived), and what specific phenomena may properly be selected out of the mass of observable data by way of illustration and example – all of which, taken together, help to make up the coherent picture or scheme or theoretical system in terms of which the analysis proceeds. Certainly, the tighter the theoretical scheme, and the more satisfactory it is in purely intellectual terms, the greater the danger that the study on which it is based will edge away from political and institutional life as the plain man knows it and take off, so to speak, for flight into the realms of scholasticism. But where there is no scheme at all, there by the same token there is no explanation and analysis – except in the historian's or journalist's sense of specific and unique event being consequent upon specific and unique incident. Since the present study is nothing if not an attempt at nailing down the general and the recurrent, the latter type of explanation is of relatively little value and the risks attendant on theorizing must, in consequence, be borne.

These difficulties are common to political analysis in all sectors of the field. Foreign policy analysis offers certain problems of its own. These stem, in part, from the difficulty of setting boundaries to the subject. The foreign policy of country A is not merely the resultant of certain processes of deliberation within the governmental institutions of A. It is also, to suggest only one of many possible addenda, a function – remote or immediate – of the foreign policies of countries B and C and D with which A interacts internationally. And the complete account of A's foreign affairs should properly include fully as detailed an account of the foreign affairs of B, C and D. But this is both beyond the bounds of normal human ability and less than crucial in a study of this (modest) scope.

But in part, too, analysis of the foreign policy processes of Britain or any other modern state entails the consideration of some matters which no academic observer can be entirely privy to. Secrecy, discretion, and – be it said – misinformation, characterize all modern diplomacy and will no doubt continue to do so until the Wilsonian millenium of open covenants of peace openly arrived at is upon us. It might, perhaps, be argued that, accordingly, only an insider who has participated personally in the processes described here over an extended period should attempt a discussion of them. Unfortunately, insiders tend to avoid the kind of overview presented here, preferring to stick to the respectable and certainly smoother furrows of autobiography, on the one hand, and the description of formal institutions, on the other. Both are valuable. Neither really deals with – still less answers – the questions with which this essay is concerned. So for all these difficulties there seemed at least minimal justification for such an attempt as this to interpret what is, without any doubt at all, an extremely intricate, if not arcane subject – even by somebody who in more senses than one stands outside the processes by which British foreign policy is actually made.

It will be noted that this essay is concerned with the *making* of foreign policy. It is not an account, still less a critique, of British foreign policy as such. Nor could it be. One could, perhaps, attempt a retrospective, historical account of what British foreign policy was on some very specific issue at a specific point in time; but one cannot talk usefully about British foreign policy in general, and in the present tense. One of the points that this book attempts to make, if only implicitly, is that there is no such animal, nor could there be. Instead, there are, so to speak, a great many policies on a great many matters, coexisting, often uncomfortably and uncertainly, at various levels of definition, priority and recognition. If an overall picture is wanted – and it is quite definitely with the overall picture that this book deals – the matter must be appropriate to being cast in terms which will be reasonably general, yet still sufficiently valid. And for such a purpose only the *process* of policy-making will serve because only it lends itself to generalizing analysis.

But if there neither is nor can be foreign policy in general,[1] there

---

[1] In contemporary Britain, at any rate. The case of a totalitarian state ruled by a megalomaniac dictator is clearly different.

is nonetheless a sense in which there is indeed much foreign policy in particular – a policy of attempting to enter the European Economic Community, or not evacuating Gibraltar, or maintaining, or not maintaining, a military presence East of Suez. One cannot therefore altogether avoid the question, precisely what does the term 'policy' signify? Dictionary definitions are often inadequate, if not misleading – e.g. 'A settled course adopted and followed by a government, institution, [etc.]' or, elsewhere, 'A course of action adopted esp. in State affairs'. These represent a quasi-legalistic, not to say old-fashioned view of the matter. The link between intention and event is not a simple causal one. A settled course is one which *ipso facto* is liable to fail. Action may be taken without a course being fully plotted, or even understood by those who, nominally, may be said to have adopted it. There is, finally, an important sense in which 'policy' is formulated by the historian, journalist or foreign opponent, rather than, necessarily, by those whom all three would agree on regarding as the policy-maker. These points, it is hoped, will be made plainer as the discussion proceeds.

If a reasonably rigorous definition is still sought, 'policy' can probably be seen most usefully as *a formulation of desired outcomes which are intended (or expected) to be consequent upon decisions adopted (or 'made') by those who have the authority (or ability) to commit the machinery of state and a significant fraction of national resources to that end.* But if one is to avoid the mires of pedanticism with any success, it is essential to see that the analytical emphasis must be consistently on the process of formulation, rather than the outcome, on the decisions, rather than the 'policy'.

*   *   *

I have been fortunate in being able to discuss a draft of this study with two friends and colleagues, Mr Peter Calvocoressi and Dr Bruce Graham, for whose comments and counsel I am most grateful. I have also been able to consult other friends whom the proprieties forbid me to name, but whose readiness to illuminate some of the less accessible corners of Whitehall puts me greatly in their debt.

D.V.

University of Sussex.
January, 1968.

I

The Problem

THE body of men who are responsible for the formulation and implementation of foreign policy are concerned, in practice, with matters over which their control is severely restricted, of which their knowledge can never be better than imperfect and which they must generally approach without the tactical and intellectual advantages of unambiguous and wholly appropriate goals.

In the main, the authority of a modern central government stops at its borders. In many cases it does not extend that far. Certain states, by virtue of the magnitude of the economic and military resources they command, or by their capacity and readiness to exploit the political and social weaknesses of their neighbours, or even of quite remote countries, may succeed in attaining a measure of influence over foreign governments which the latter may be unable to shake off. By sedulous and uninhibited exploitation of economic dependence, or military inferiority, or subversive elements, or of any other variety or combination of carrot and stick they may succeed in extending their authority into the nominal jurisdiction of others. But it is of the essence of the contemporary state system that such extra-territorial authority is uncertain, often no more than fleeting. Even in such classic modern cases as that of the Soviet paramountcy in Eastern Europe in the first decade after the Second World War, or of the milder and relatively benevolent paramountcy of the United States in parts of Latin America, the possibility of rebellion and escape can never be removed. And, indeed, the successful perpetuation of such paramountcy by nonforcible means depends, in practice, on a continual process of adjustment and reconciliation to new and undesired departures from previously established norms.

Broadly speaking, the multiplication of sovereign states that has occurred since the end of the Second World War[1] and the continuing conflict between the three greatest powers have had the combined

---

[1] There are just over 140 at the time of writing.

effect of reducing the influence which any one state – however powerful – may exercise over any other. Certainly for a state of the second
rank like Britain there is today little room left for manoeuvre as of
right and by fiat in the manner familiar to us from accounts of the
carving up of much of Asia and Africa by the European powers in the
eighteenth and nineteenth centuries. Only the greatest and the
smallest powers remain comparatively uninhibited about the use of
force. This may change, but for the time being and for as far as can
be discerned, the instruments of foreign policy for states in the intermediate range on the scale of human and material resources (e.g.
Britain, France, Italy, Japan and West Germany) must be preponder-
antly diplomatic rather than forcible, aimed at the minds of foreign
leaders rather than at the ribs and stomachs of their subjects. Military force, economic pressure, psychological warfare, cloak and dagger
operations and the like can assuredly all coexist with traditional diplomacy. But their function is principally one of *deterrence* by provid-
ing last-ditch, physical defences or, alternatively, one of serving as
marginal supplements and reinforcements to overt diplomacy. Since
the failure of the Suez Operation in 1956 the reluctance of such secondary powers to initiate the employment of forcible instruments of
policy in foreign conflicts has greatly increased. This has by no means
entirely excluded their use – as witness, for example, British military intervention on the side of Malaysia in the Indonesian-Malaysian
confrontation and the attempt to employ economic pressure in the
conflict with Rhodesia. But in both these cases a great deal was done
to avoid and postpone their employment for as long as possible. And
further, when employed, they were employed reluctantly and with
the express and explicit desire to return to non-forcible methods of
implementing policy as soon as possible.

However, irrespective of the nature of the instrument – diplomatic
or forcible – selected to further chosen policy, the decision to employ it normally flows from a certain appreciation of the circumstances
to which that instrument is thought applicable. Such appreciations,
or assessments, or estimates – as they are variously called – are the
raw material of all foreign policy-making, whatever the solutions, or
actions, or inaction ultimately resolved upon. They, in turn, are built
up out of the data flowing into the central policy-making machinery
in the form of embassy dispatches, telegrams, press reports and intelligence material grafted on to the material available or in prepara-
tion at home – reports on diplomatic talks conducted at the foreign
ministry itself, the work of official analysts, the relevant papers of
other ministries and such historical and archival material as is on tap.

Perfectly comprehensive and wholly reliable information about the external environment, the world beyond its own sovereign jurisdiction, is beyond the reach of any government. No matter how widespread its network of diplomatic missions, how much it invests in its intelligence services, how diligent its officials and how efficient the central administration at home, much will escape its observers, or be misinterpreted or neglected by its analysts, or be beyond assimilation by the key policy-making personnel. Confronted with a multiplicity of phenomena – political, economic, military, social, administrative – which may be thought to bear some *prima facie* relation to the behaviour of governments, societies and influential personalities in each one of the 140 sovereign states (and in a further group of dependent territories) the administrators of foreign relations must insist upon selectivity. If they do not, their colleagues in the ministry of finance will surely do so for them: the collection and assimilation of information is costly and time-consuming and unless bounds are set on the categories and quantities of data no useful bounds can be set on the costs in time and money. The governments of the United States and the Soviet Union are sometimes suspected of wishing to know 'everything', of seeking fully comprehensive coverage of the world beyond their borders, at least in so far as topics may have political implications. Perhaps they do. Yet this would seem to be an inherently over-ambitious, not to say doubtful undertaking, even for the superpowers. In the first place, even the term 'political' is too loose to serve as a guide-line. There are very few matters which do not have, actually or potentially, some political content: agriculture, science, industry, national health, the crime rate, and state education are all matters of passionate interest to some element of the population of each country and all are subjects for which some component of the state administration is responsible. Affairs in all these (and many other) fields are therefore liable to influence the pattern of national politics through the interplay of political pressures and rivalries. Each has some bearing on the state's prosperity and military potential. And the examination of each such field will assist in the interpretation of its political affairs and prospects as a whole – which for the foreign observer is almost as important a test of relevance. The views and personalities of bankers, parliamentarians, admirals and chief constables may therefore all excite the interest of foreign observers almost as greatly as those of senior officials and political leaders. But it is also immediately obvious that for the most part the condition of industry for example, must merit greater attention than that of the schools, and that the views of admirals are *prima facie* more enlightening on matters of external policy than those of policemen, however senior, and that some parliamentarians are more interesting, better informed and closer to the seats of power than others. In brief, the line that must be drawn, somewhere, even by the greatest and wealthiest and most inquisitive of powers, must be such as to help make a practical distinction between the significant and the trivial, between the topic which is highly revealing and that which is marginally informative, between the informant who is manifestly possessed of both information and insight and the contact who is at best a good random exemplar of his class and condition. This is by no means easy to do.

The difficulty is akin to one which pervades 'quality' journalism: out of the mass of possibilities what items of news are actually worth printing; and what stories are worth following up repeatedly over an extended period? Much may be decided by reference to traditional practice. Some newspapers habitually carry specific classes of stories (e.g. the Court page of the *Times*) that are anything but newsworthy in the narrow sense of the term. Diplomatic services tend to traditional practice in much the same manner: a great deal of their time is spent in customary activities which are then reported on in a customary form, semi-automatically. The problem of on what – or on whom – to concentrate active attention remains. Is the seemingly dull and uninspired official or parliamentarian in fact closer to an understanding of the political processes and likely behaviour of his country than his seniors? Is the commercial banker's gloomy (or cheerful) prognostication more reliable than the cheerful (or gloomy) outlook of the central banker or treasury official? Whom does one cultivate; whose comments does one report; and, above all, which line of investigation does one follow up?

Again, the problem facing the diplomatic observer can be compared to that of a diplomatic historian working with insufficient access to documents. The gaps in knowledge must be filled in by a process of informal guess-work, by reference to some general pattern of events which is itself unverifiable because it is in great measure the creation of the observer himself. It is indeed the function of the intelligence services (at any rate, their ambition) to provide the 'documents' – which is to say, those items of information which are both truly revelatory of the inner workings and purposes of the government under observation and entirely reliable in character themselves. Yet in the world of political[2] decision-making the search for 'documents' can be a chase after phantoms. There may be no 'documents' in a literal sense, or they may be seriously incomplete. The decision of today

[2] The case of military decision-making is somewhat different.

may be upset tomorrow. The observed are equally observers. Pieces of information may be well attested to, yet they may conflict in content. The intentions of governments, even where known, even where clearly defined, cannot be entirely reliable indicators of future behaviour because actions may ultimately be determined by external factors and involuntary decisions. The factor of irrationality, a possible tendency to wish-fulfilment or to 'over-reaction' to events, and, above all, the play of 'the contingent and the unforseen' upon the subject on which interest is focused in the tangle of relations between any single given state and all others – all these must be taken into account.

These complexities serve to underline the significance of what for the simple, practical purposes of the managers of the state's foreign policy-making machinery are the two central characteristics of their external environment. Firstly, there is the impossibility of proceeding to an interpretation of events without going through the intermediate process of harsh and continuous selection of both the topics on which interest is to be concentrated and the data which is to be fitted into the picture, or estimate, or assessment on which policy is to be based or in terms of which pre-conceived policy is to be justified. And secondly, there is the indeterminancy of the foreign political scene and the practical[3] impossibility of ascribing causal relationships and connections between perceived phenomena of sufficient reliability to eliminate, or at least very sharply reduce, dependence on intuition, on the partially formulated 'lessons' of experience, on precedent, and on such mystery elements of public affairs as 'leadership', 'public opinion', 'prestige', and 'honour'.

The tasking of formulating a valid and relevant picture of the foreign scene is often likened to that of fitting together the pieces of a jig-saw puzzle. But it is not nearly as simple as that. If the simile is to serve at all, it must be remembered that only a fraction of the pieces are available at any given time, that none fit smoothly into others, that the player must match the pieces according to a conception of the whole that is of his own invention, and that no two players will ever arrive at precisely the same result. Moreover, the individual pieces change in shape and colouring as the game proceeds; and, in practice, a very large number of players will be attempting the same exercise simultaneously, some seeing only a minor section of the puzzle, others seeing more, but mostly at so great a distance from the individual pieces that the outlines of those they perceive may be blurred almost beyond clear recognition.

[3] This is not intended as a comment on the much wider question of determinism in the ultimate sense of the term as understood by philosophers.

The selection, verification, comparison and interpretation of environmental phenomena is, in fact, inseparable from the twin processes of identifying the key variables in the situation which confronts one and the explicit (and in some cases implicit) definition of one's own political goals. The importance attached, say, to the internal politics of a foreign state will depend in great measure on the view taken of their likely impact on that state's behaviour. The interest taken by state A in state B's industrial affairs will probably be geared in some degree to the interest A takes in B's military power; and this, in turn, may depend on the political relations between the two states, or on the assessment of B's own diplomatic goals, or on the prospects for war or for peace between the two states, or on the desirability of trade in armaments between them. Certain topics are, of course, of traditional, habitual interest – the military establishments, the state of the economy, the central rivalries in the domestic political arena, the state of public opinion, the views of political leaders, and the state's international circumstances – because long experience has shown, or is thought to have shown, that knowledge of these serves as a guide both to the possibilities open to a given state to pursue internationally and to the goals it is in fact likely to pursue. Political analysts tend to look for variables such as these in the belief that they help to reveal what a foreign government's international behaviour is likely to be, somewhat in the manner that economists look for economic indicators such as the growth rate, the employment rate and the balance of payments. But here few of the phenomena are quantifiable, if any, and, as has been suggested, they are too numerous, too uncertain and divisible into too many barely related categories for the process to carry even the surface conviction that is the usual attribute of purely economic studies.

But along with the identification and investigation of the key political variables in foreign states must go the process of definition and re-definition of the state's key goals in its foreign affairs. The distinction between the relevant and the irrelevant, between the important and the trivial, between matters which merit priority treatment and those which can be handled at leisure or postponed *sine die*, and between topics which must be referred to the highest authority and those which can be safely dealt with at the lowest rungs of the hierarchy cannot be made by simple reference to the intrinsic character of the question, problem, event or proposition that has come into the ken of the machine. In foreign affairs all is relative – relative to one's own needs, position, dangers, hopes and purposes. The making of foreign policy is founded on ego-centricity. This is to say that, given the character of the contemporary international system of sovereign states and the conventions upon which it rests, a foreign policy can only make sense in so far as it is calculated to advance, or at least to defend, the interests of the state concerned. Even where the policy is projected in moral or social terms of general relevance and validity – such as peace, human prosperity and political democracy – and even where it entails some sacrifice or surrender on the part of the society in whose name it is advanced, it must be fundamentally self-seeking to be politically and logically tenable. Alternatively, it must at the very least be justifiable in terms of an avoidance of a greater sacrifice or injury. In other words, peace for all must entail peace for X. Surrender of territory, for example, must be arguably preferable to prospective annihilation. A policy which is not self-seeking in this sense is either self-contradictory, or treasonable, or founded on error.

If there is no other logical framework but this in which a foreign policy can be conceived, there is by the same token no other standard by which it can be judged. A policy that advances the security and well-being of the state in whose name it is pursued may be adjudged successful; one which does not, a failure. But a standard by which to judge policy is not itself a policy. Such standards and judgments are too general to serve as practical guides through the international jungle. In any case, they can reflect no more than *minimal* state purposes: the mere distinction between success and failure is not in itself a measure of success (or of failure, for that matter). The principal stuff of international politics is made up, whether one likes it or not, of instances of more far-reaching and ambitious, even maximalist, and yet fully rational and self-consistent plans of campaign – policies of aggression, territorial aggrandizement, imperialism (simple, neo-, quasi- and crypto-), and striving for regional, if not world hegemony. It is therefore the concrete and specific goals or set of goals in a concrete and specific situation that must be investigated and laid bare in each case and these will naturally vary greatly from society to society and from situation to situation. They will vary too in potential clarity of definition, no less than in content.

Few governments are clear in their collective mind about their basic purposes and foreign observers intent on understanding what they are about may make the common error of ascribing consistency and rationality to a pattern of administration which owes much more to chance, emotion and intuition. The interests of the 'state' may mean no more, in practice, than the interests of an oligarchy, or of a single individual. The well-being of one sector of the national community may be incompatible with that of another. The 'national interest' as a portmanteau term has its uses, but it may be beyond precise definition both by those intimately concerned with its pursuit and by the historian in retrospect. Issues in foreign relations may be resolved, in practice, by reference to nominally 'domestic' factors – those, for example, which may be thought to determine the future internal prospects of the party or personalities in power. In short, very many of the uncertainties, conflicts, incompatibilities of interest, differences of assessment and struggles for clear formulation of problems and policies that characterize the external environment are to be found repeated within the state in new, but hardly less tractable forms.

Ideally, the functions of the foreign policy-maker are the reconciliation of external and internal interests, the resolution of incompatibilities between policies directed at discrete targets, choice between partially or wholly different assessments and interpretations, and the setting of goals in terms of which the administrative machinery is to operate. In the abstract, the locus of his activity is the point where all the lines of communication and pressure, foreign and domestic, intersect. It is he, not exclusively, but more notably than any other participant in the policy-making process as a whole, who provides the non-verifiable, unsystematic, intuitive and normative components of interpretation and policy. And up to a point his role may be so defined. It is the policy-makers as a group who give style and direction to the administrative machine that feeds them with data in various states of digestion and executes their instructions. But equally, they may fail to give it clear direction – because the complexities of the environment overwhelm them intellectually, or because the machine is inadequate, or because the objective problems that beset them are beyond treatment and manipulation.

At best, a great part of a perfect foreign policy-making machine would be somewhat like a computer: vast quantities of data would be fed into it, to emerge subsequently in manageable, pre-determined groups with all the conceivable consequences of each experienced and predicted event duly worked out and compared. But both the problem of programming the computer and that of the final choice of the alternative courses of action would remain to be dealt with. The machine can assist the decision-makers. It cannot replace them.

At the same time it would be wrong to see the policy-making machinery in its entirety as a form of map-making and the process of foreign policy-making as something equivalent to the work of a reconnaissance patrol seeking out the enemy and simultaneously plotting the optimum route of advance for the major body of troops. Political reconnaissance is an essential element of the process, but it does not fully cover it. The policy-making machinery of state is concerned no less with *altering* the topography in which it must operate – by open persuasion, by guile or by force. The questions it must continually ask itself are not only what, in the circumstances, is to be done and how may it be done well, but also how may the circumstances be changed, how may advantages be created and disadvantages minimized. Foreign policy-making is both extrospective and introspective. It is concerned both with the external environment and with what the state may do about it. The ancient simile of the ship of state has more than a little truth in it. The captain must assuredly set his course according to the configuration of the coast and the strength and direction of the winds and currents, but he must also navigate in a manner compatible with the power of his engines, the strength of the ship's hull, and the availability of fuel. A daring commander supported by a loyal and efficient crew and equipped with up-to-date charts and radar can accomplish a great deal; but he must beware of venturing into regions where icebergs proliferate or where he is in danger of running short of supplies.

So before going on to consider the structure, components, procedures and practice of the British foreign policy-making machine, it is necessary to review briefly what Britain's international circumstances are and give some account at least of the major problems with which the machine is expected to cope and at which foreign policy is chiefly directed.[4]

---

[4] A review, such as the one which follows, cannot be anything but a review of the past. Moreover, it will be dated, if only marginally, by the time it is in print. Chapter II should be read, therefore, essentially as an account of the *kind* of problems which British foreign policy-makers have been faced with since the war and the *kind* of dilemmas that they have had to resolve. Some of these problems and dilemmas will, on present showing, be with them for some years to come; others may not. But all in all, because both a nation's international circumstances and the patterns of individual behaviour, while being subject to continuous change alter very slowly, the sort of retrospective analysis that follows should be of some help when we come to consider contemporary practice. There is, in any case, no alternative. The present and the future are in the strict sense, unknowable and we are left with what we know or comprehend about the past on which – and with which – to build.

II

The External Environment

'England seeks no quarrels' – EYRE CROWE

VIEWED summarily and without regard for past splendours modern Britain cannot but be reckoned a very considerable and well-endowed member of the contemporary (1968) international community. The security of the United Kingdom is underwritten by the greatest of all military powers under a military alliance system to which Britain herself contributes one of the most elaborate and costly defence establishments in the world. She is a permanent, veto-wiedling member of the Security Council of the United Nations. She retains military and territorial footholds in many parts of the world, notably in Western Europe and in the Mediterranean, but also – at least until 1971, if not beyond – in the Persian Gulf and in South-east Asia. She is a member of NATO, CENTO and SEATO. All of this gives her a voice and, on occasion, some real political leverage in the affairs of other nations and other regions in a measure such as would not normally fall to a state of the middle rank situated off the north-west coast of Europe. She is the principal member of the Commonwealth – a fact which can, at the very least, serve to facilitate diplomatic contacts with a large number of states. She is the principal trading partner of a fair number and variety of countries ranging geographically from the Irish Republic to New Zealand and a very significant trading partner, banker, supplier of capital, economic and technical aid and military weapons to a very much greater number of nations in all five continents. She possesses such not inconsiderable psychological advantages as political greatness in the recent past, scientific, technological and cultural accomplishments of the highest order, a stable domestic society, a prestigious diplomatic service and her population's own natural fluency in the world's major commercial and scientific language.

Quantitatively, Britain comes eleventh in world order of population, but third in production and consumption of energy. She is first in merchant shipping,[1] third in production of coal, second in the building and launching of ships, fifth in production of both iron and steel, seventh in production of cement, fifth in production of automobiles and fifth again in the production of radio and television receivers. She is the world's second greatest trading nation. In Gross Domestic Product per capita – a rough indicator of standard of living – Britain ranks seventh. Gloomy prognostications about declining British material strength have been made continuously since the end of the Second World War and it has been argued very seriously that Britain will ultimately fall far behind other great industrial states (Japan, West Germany, France and Italy) with which she is on roughly equal terms of size and wealth today. And certainly it is hard to contest the common assertion that Britain is no longer possessed of the almost world-wide political and military influence that was hers at the beginning of the century. Nevertheless, if one takes a simple, cross-sectional view of contemporary Britain, rather than one embodying a speculative extrapolation from her current condition into the future, if, in other words, one considers the balance sheet of national advantages and disadvantages as it appears in the late 1960's, rather than the use made of them and the seeming pattern of their future evolution, the wholly ineluctable difficulties faced by Britain are not of startling dimensions. They may arouse disquiet, but not fear or despair.

The security of Britain is under no visible – certainly no immediate – threat. Her geographical position insulates her from most of the familiar consequences of propinquity with other nations: she does not live in the shadow of a great and powerful neighbour (like Poland, Mexico and Burma for example) and now that the Irish problem is practically dead she has no problems of irredenta and disputed territory of her own (like Germany and India and very many other states). Britain is troubled by no guerrilla or subversive movements, not even a legal communist party of any consequence. Such armed conflicts as Britain has been engaged in since the end of the war have been with geographically remote and, for the most part, very much weaker national forces: the Palestinian Jews, the Malayan terrorists, the Kikuyu, the Greek Cypriots, the Egyptians and the Indonesians. None of these have threatened the security of the United Kingdom as such. None have ever succeeded in allying themselves more than superficially or fleetingly with powers that could. Only the Cold War with the Soviet Union has contained elements of real, if only potential, danger, but here, in view of Britain's alliance with the state possessing

[1] The aggregate tonnage of ships flying Liberia's flag of convenience is now marginally greater than that of Britain's merchant fleet.

the preponderance of military force, it is precisely in this respect that she has been best protected.

Britain's chief structural weaknesses and difficulties, well known and exhaustively documented and debated for twenty years, lie elsewhere. The heart of the matter is that the United Kingdom is small in area and densely populated and that her share of the blessings of nature is severely limited both quantitatively and qualitatively. There is insufficient arable land to feed more than approximately half her population and the only substantial domestic source of energy is coal in an age that gives priority to petroleum. The contribution of natural gas and nuclear energy to total needs is, however, a rapidly growing one. Britain has some domestic sources of iron (annual production is a third that of Sweden's), but hardly any of the other important minerals: no bauxite, no chrome, no copper, infinitesimal supplies of gold, very little lead, no manganese, no nickel, barely any silver and very little tin. The well known consequence of these and other shortages is the overwhelming importance of foreign trade to her economic prosperity[2] with all that extensive foreign trade necessarily implies: fragility of the economy as a whole, a chronic and probably ineradicable balance of payments problem, and a very high degree of governmental sensitivity to the economic aspects of policy questions, both domestic and external, in all spheres of administration. Hence too the profound, almost unparalleled influence on the making of British foreign policy of those ministers and officials who are concerned with economic and financial affairs over and above their general responsibility for the supervision of government expenditure in all spheres.

There are thus no more than two spheres in which the foreign policy of the United Kingdom may be said to be decisively dictated by her basic circumstances in the sense that the goals of policy should emerge simply and unmistakably from a consideration of the major elements of the environment in which the British policy-makers must operate. These are the physical defence of the United Kingdom and the maintenance of her economic (and hence social) welfare. Regard for the first is at the root of Britain's membership in NATO and, more particularly, her 'special relationship' with the United States. Concern for the second pervades all British politics, both internal and external, and has lead to the most spectacular departure from the

[2] In absolute terms the United States is the world's greatest trading nation and Britain the second. Yet while Britain's Gross National Product is only one-seventh of the American, her exports of goods and services total approximately *two-thirds* of those of the United States.

norm in recent times – the successive applications in 1961 and 1967 to join the European Economic Community. But the briefest glance at some of the foreign questions, problems, difficulties and conflicts that have beset British leaders in recent years reveals that Britain's external environment – conceived as the sum of those elements of the international political scene as a whole which impinge, or are thought to impinge, on British interests and therefore to require action through some instrument of British policy – is very much more complex.

This complexity arises partly out of the fact that modern British governments find themselves, on accession to power, confronted not by a political *tabula rasa,* but by a great accumulation of established practice and doctrine among their officials and of undertakings, arrangements and continuing conflicts which they have the greatest difficulty in ignoring or circumventing even where they are judged irrelevant to major governmental purposes. The particular difficulty for Britain is that the steady liquidation of the empire from 1947 onwards has not been accompanied by a proportionate clearing away of such accumulated practice, doctrine and commitments, while the parallel waning of Britain's material strength and influence that has been the major consequence of the liquidation of empire has made each successive step in the dismantling of the empire and the establishment of new alignments proportionately more burdensome.

In part too, no doubt, the complexity of Britain's external environment reflects an important and characteristic feature of all international affairs – as of other fields of social activity – namely, the impossibility of fully isolating any given event or phenomenon, and therefore, by extension, of isolating a specific political act such that its effects be sharply confined to the issue at which it is directed.

It is thus noteworthy, for example, that Britain has been recently involved, and heavily involved, in at least three major conflicts, each of which led to the employment of force (military in two cases, economic in the third), but each of which was entered into unwillingly and in none of which was Britain advancing or even very notably defending a clear and major national interest. Furthermore, though each conflict made heavy material and political demands on the country, in no case could a favourable outcome be expected to leave Britain in a total situation which was an improvement upon that obtaining prior to the precipitation of the conflict.

From 1963 until the overthrow of President Sukarno in March, 1966, she had been engaged in limited, but substantial warfare with Indonesia which was attempting to bring down the new Malaysian state by means of armed 'confrontation'. Britain was, in fact, explicitly obliged to come to Malaysia's assistance under the terms of the 1957 Anglo-Malayan Defence Agreement, and some 58,000 British troops were ultimately committed to her defence.

The essential virtue of the Defence Agreement was that it allowed Britain to keep her strategic reserve in Malaya and Singapore and so make a continuing presence 'east of Suez' possible. But by 1963 interest in an east of Suez posture had greatly waned. In any case the effectiveness of the reserve was clearly open to question. Britain's military presence failed to deter Indonesia and the end of the fighting came about principally as a result of internal changes in that country and was only marginally related to the progress of the small war in Borneo. And since the end of the operation was followed in less than two years by a final decision to abandon the east of Suez posture, the total effort seems to have been expended on a fulfilment of anachronistic obligations rather than on a reinforcement of dispositions for the future.

In 1966 Britain proclaimed her intention of granting independence to Aden within a new South Arabian Federation. This had the effect of substantially intensifying the terror campaign waged by Egyptian- and Yemeni-backed radical nationalists in Aden intent on wresting the political initiative from the British-backed, conservative South Arabian government and ensuring their own control of the territory upon the departure of the British. Reluctance to hand the territory over to the nationalists, or simply to depart and leave the local rivals to fight over the spoils, was compounded of a variety of elements. These ranged from a belief in the general value of keeping undertakings (in this case to the local conservative rulers and their allies among the Adeni merchants) no matter how burdensome they had become, to the perceived advantages of bolstering the opponents of President Nasser (these same rulers and their allies in other parts of Arabia) and, so contributing to the maintenance of the political and economic *status quo* in the Middle East and East Africa. But the prize for which the contestants themselves were struggling – Aden itself – was one which Britain had already renounced. And if British policy was primarily aimed at keeping Egyptain and Iraqi influence out of South Arabia and the Persian Gulf it would clearly be more difficult to implement once Britain herself had evacuated her forces from the best base available for the purpose.

Britain's most painful and intractable conflict in this period was, however, with the group of white Rhodesians who had proclaimed 'unilateral' independence in November, 1965 in the face of almost universal disapproval and protest and to the great embarrassment of the suzerain British government. In some respects the problem was analogous to that of the American colonies' declaration of independence in 1776, the difference being that this time the 'Indians' were a recognized, constituent element of the problem and had, moreover, the advantage of the political, though not material, support of a great many foreign powers, among them most members of the Commonwealth. Despite the latter's urgings, Britain refused to employ armed force against Ian Smith and his colleagues.[3] But every other conceivable weapon of coercion from limited economic sanctions enforced by naval blockade to psychological warfare with the help of the BBC was employed. Every possible constitutional formula was explored. At one stage the British government went so far as to offer the Smith government an Act of Union with the United Kingdom as an inducement to return to the fold. But the obstacles were formidable. One reason why the UN-authorized economic sanctions were less effective than they might have been was the unwillingness of South Africa to cooperate – on the understandable grounds, among others, that success in cowing the white Rhodesians by these means would encourage attempts to employ them subsequently against South Africa. In this respect, given the South African contribution in trade, gold and return on investments to the British economy, Britain's position was particularly hard, her conduct, not surprisingly, shifting, and her intentions uncertain, even ambiguous.

Yet what is particularly striking about the Rhodesian affair is, once again, the absence of any clear and direct United Kingdom interest in the downfall of the Smith regime.

A great many hard, political arguments could be advanced to explain and justify British policy, over and above the formal reasons for asserting sovereignty and the weighty ethical grounds for refusing to condone the handing over of the overwhelming majority of Africans to a statistically insignificant minority of whites. Opposition to Smith was essential if the Commonwealth was to be held together – if only by verbal bonds – and failure to act at all might have created a golden opportunity for violent subversion at the behest of the Russians, or the Chinese, or the Algerians, or the Egyptains, or of any one of the radical political movements of black Africa. But it remains that for Britain herself the grounds for opposing the Smith regime were essen-

---

[3] Some observers believed at the time that the key factor was the over-commitment of troops in Borneo and Aden then obtaining and Britain's consequent material inability to deal with additional arenas of military conflict. The evidence for this is slight and it appears reasonably clear that the decisive arguments against the employment of force were, in fact, political and economic.

tially remote from the realities of life in the United Kingdom. They were legal, historical, even ethical, only marginally economic, if at all, and political and strategic only in the sense that the fate of these distant territories could only be linked to that of Great Britain by long and intricate chains of speculative argument. For the parties on the spot, on the other hand, the issues in Rhodesia – as in Borneo and Aden – were direct and *un*speculative; the retention or attainment of political power, the advancement of allies, the displacement of enemies the immediate welfare and security of individuals and social and ethnic groups, relative freedom to pursue policies of their own devising, and so forth.

Such involvement in conflicts which relate only indirectly and speculatively to the rock-bottom requirements of national safety and prosperity is the traditional hall-mark of a power with 'world-wide interests', of membership in that class of powers which the Victorians called 'regulating states'. But clearly, the more widespread the sphere of interests, the greater must be the resources required to cope with them and the stronger must be the determination underlying the effort to sustain them. For on the one hand, the attempt to sustain world-wide interests leads to the discovery of secondary and tertiary interests that must be upheld in their turn and a tendency to ever greater and ever deeper involvement in subsidiary theatres of operation and concern – the acquisition of distant bases to sustain forces to protect established interests in still more distant regions, for example, and a consequent inflation of the political, economic and military investment required to support aggregate foreign policy. On the other hand, the greater the geographical and conceptual remoteness of each new subject of concern as it appears on the mental horizon of the home population, the greater will be the intricacy, if not artificiality, of the arguments that must be advanced by the metropolitan government to justify the expenditure of life and treasure which political action in distant parts almost inevitably entails. Broadly speaking, therefore, a government's freedom to play a major role on the international stage – or, in alternative terms, the extent to which its leaders will be free to indulge their extra-national ambitions – tends to vary with the sum of human and material resources at its command, with the authority it can exert over its metropolitan population, and with the character of the discrete problems which face it overseas. Each of these variables is, of course, functionally related to the other two: the greater the resources of the state, the smaller the consequent burden on the metropolitan population; the greater the authority of the government over that population, the smaller will be the factor of effective popular discontent; and the milder the problems facing the metropolitan state, the smaller will be the required investment of resources. Greatly simplified, therefore, Britain's difficulties in sustaining her role as a 'regulating state' in the world can be seen as having followed a radical change in all three parameters: her resources have shrunk – both absolutely and relative to the problems she has had to face, the evolution of the external environment has been such as to increase by several orders of magnitude the difficulties of maintaining political influence overseas, and the population at home has been (or has been judged to be) increasingly reluctant to make the requisite sacrifices. And as foreign affairs in general and Britain's international prestige in particular play only a marginal role, if any, in contemporary British domestic politics,[4] political leaders have generally tended, and with good reason, to avoid dynamic and assertive courses of action in the foreign sphere. The great exception to this latter rule of conduct in the recent past is, of course, the attempt to re-assert British authority in the Middle East that occurred in 1956. And significantly enough, among the causes of the collapse of the Suez campaign was the belated recognition by the Eden government of the great economic sacrifice successful completion of the operation would require of Britain and of the political impossibility, or undesirability, of inducing the British public to pay a great price for an uncertain and – to many – disproportionate end.

Put in cruder terms still, there is neither the will in contemporary Britain (except in small and politically insignificant circles) to maintain the role of a world power, nor the resources to do so. The liquidation of the Empire that began with the grant of independence to India in 1947 is now almost complete. Only the vestiges of empire continue to trouble Britain and, as the examples of Malaysia, Aden and Rhodesia suggest, to require what cannot but appear disproportionate attention.

In the past Britain's status as a world power was very largely a function of her empire and of her leadership of the 'white dominions'. But at the same time she derived much of her capacity to maintain her colonies and her political leadership over the sovereign members of the imperial system from the empire itself. In 1947 this reciprocal relationship broke down. The surrender of India probably freed Britain from the prospect of an intolerable burden, but it also had the ultimate effect of reducing very greatly her capacity to cater for the defence of her remaining dependencies and allies on the shores

[4] Cf. Chapter IV.

of the Indian ocean and beyond. Inability to guarantee the physical security of Australia and New Zealand (a responsibility now largely assumed by the United States) has, in turn, fundamentally altered their relationship with Britain. And taken together these and other changes have greatly reduced Britain's total political and military resources in the international arena.

A second difficulty is that some of the residual ex-imperial interests bear on other interests which do continue to be undeniably central to the security and welfare of the United Kingdom. Thus Britain's remaining presence in South-east Asia is believed by some to be worth keeping up, if only for the sake of the incremental leverage it is said to give Britain in Washington. Even if the Wilson Government was right to decide in January 1968 that the balance of political and economic advantage, both external and domestic, lay in abandoning the great political/military salient of Singapore, it was always clear that the consequences of withdrawal could not be wholly advantageous. It is therefore not altogether inconceivable that the decision to leave by the end of 1971 may be reversed if a new government comes to power before then.

It is for this reason, among others, that there has been no uniformity of behaviour on the part of the British Government in its discarding of overseas territories and that no post-war government has found it possible to deal with the problem in a fully consistent manner.[5] The liquidation of an empire is not without its suicidal aspect and it is natural that there be counter-pressures to arrest the process ('Stopping the rot')[6] or to slow it down.

The variety and complexity of discrete problems and the even more intricate interplay between them with which makers of British external policy continue to be faced are by no means restricted to what might be termed the overseas penumbra of the British external environment. They are to be found almost equally in the inner, umbral sector of fundamental, non-negotiable and unquestionable interests: national security and economic warfare. The objective difficulty of defining and pursuing a wholly satisfactory policy such that progress in respect of one problem implies no retreat or unwanted complication in respect of another (as has been the case, for example, in the consistent, but mutually incompatible efforts by Britain to keep on reason-

---

[5] Contrast the withdrawal from India, Burma and Ceylon with that from the Middle East.

[6] Sir Alec Douglas-Home at the Conservative Party Conference, Brighton, October, 1967.

ably good terms with both the radical Arab states of the Middle East who have the preponderance of political influence and trouble-making capacity and with the conservative Arab states in whose domains lies the bulk of the oil)[7] is by no means exclusively a function of the attempt to pursue a role as an internationally influential power, one of the world's 'regulating states'. It is to be found in almost the same degree of intensity in those spheres where simple, straightforward and mutually compatible formulations of British external policy would appear to be, on the face of it, most easily arrived at. Indeed, the really crucial policy dilemmas for contemporary Britain arise out of the degree to which the pursuit of national security (conceived in politico-military terms) and the pursuit of national welfare (conceived in socio-economic terms) have turned out to be significantly – though perhaps not wholly – incompatible with each other. In part, this is a consequence of Britain's international situation as it has evolved since the Second World War. But this incompatibility is also a consequence of the characteristic processes by which foreign policy is made in Britain.[8] And it is to the task of reconciling the mutually incompatible elements of these two major facets of British foreign policy as a whole that a great deal of the attention of the policy-making machinery is devoted. Two notable and typical examples of this incompatibility may be cited.

The first example centres on the problem of the cost of defence in terms of economic resources. Absolute British expenditure on defence is very high (estimated at £2,218 million for 1967/68) and is likely to remain at about that level for some years to come. As a proportion of national resources it is very high too (estimated at about 6.8 per cent of GNP), but will probably fall slightly in the future. All in all, Britain's expenditure is, in absolute terms, roughly on a par with what is believed to be China's; and in both absolute and relative terms is exceeded only by that of Russia and the United States among members of NATO and the Warsaw Pact. After Social Security it is the largest item of public expenditure. And since, up to a point, a pound spent on defence may be considered a pound unspent on health, education, highways, regional development and the like – all of which may be regarded as investments in the economy which will duly re-

---

[7] Thus while Britain has desired to assist the 'conservatives' to take over in South Arabia she consistently refused to give them defence guarantees (on the Malayan model) for fear of offending the 'radicals' and embroiling herself still further in Arab affairs. But the enmity of the radicals was ensured in any case by the systematic efforts to assist the conservatives to pre-empt them.

[8] Cf. Chapter V.

pay themselves, while the bulk of defence expenditure will not – such a rate of defence expenditure entails a large net loss to the economy. Furthermore, the deployment of forces overseas (particularly in Germany, the Middle East and South-east Asia) and the reliance on the United States for supplies of certain components of the major weapons systems (notably Polaris missiles and Phantom aircraft) entail a very heavy expenditure, all of it overseas and much of it in foreign currency. Together the two classes of expenditure account annually for some £350 million.

To be sure, there are compensatory factors. There is the fundamental consideration that defence of the realm is a pre-condition of social welfare and that it is therefore absurd to regard the two as entirely contradictory. There is also the role of defence industry and technology as a stimulant to industrial technology as a whole with valuable 'spin-off' effects on the civil economy, particularly in such fields as nuclear energy, electronics, and the aero-space industry. Nevertheless, at the margin, there is an inevitable conflict between the two sets of considerations and therefore parallel and endemic conflict between those professionally concerned to buttress defensive dispositions and military support for foreign policy and those who are professionally concerned with the health and growth of the national economy alone. This incompatibility between major national goals as their attainment must be worked out in practice can be seen very clearly in the case of the British military presence in Germany.

Unlike the Far Eastern strategic reserve or the relatively small military forces available for employment in the Persian Gulf – both of which, as has been said, are to be withdrawn in 1971 – the 55,000 troops which are Britain's permanent commitment to NATO fulfil a role which has always been conceived of in terms of the immediate security of the United Kingdom. Put very simply, the only readily apparent, contemporary threat to the physical security of Britain, either by direct attack or by attack on those countries in western Europe the conquest or political domination of which by a hostile power would fundamentally alter Britain's strategic situation, emanates from Russia. The somewhat more remote contingency of a resurgence of German aggressive nationalism would also constitute a danger, though a lesser one. An alliance between a hostile Soviet Union and a resurgent Germany re-unified on that very basis, i.e. of an *Ost-politik* – an even more remote contingency, but still not one that can be dismissed out of hand – would constitute the greatest danger of all. In contrast, none of the other European states, nor any of the transatlantic, African or Asian states, not even China, appear likely to present a military threat to Britain in any readily conceivable contingency whatsoever. In other words, Britain must be defended in Europe. The instrument of her defence in Europe against the superior forces of the hostile and potentially hostile power that do, or may, confront it is the North Atlantic Treaty Organization. In the language of the 1966 *Defence Review*,

' . . . the first purpose of our armed forces will be to defend the freedom of the British people. The security of these islands still depends primarily on preventing war in Europe. For this reason, we regard the continuation of the North Atlantic alliance as vital to our survival.'[9]

The military effectiveness of the North Atlantic Alliance rests on two key components: the capacity of the Americans to strike at the heart of the Soviet Union with nuclear weapons – the deterrent; and the multi-national land forces armed with both conventional and tactical nuclear weapons and deployed along the East-West frontiers – the 'trip-wire'. The strategic role of the first component is one of terrifying simplicity – to demonstrate that any armed conflict can lead to massive destruction within Soviet territory. The role of the second component is more complex. The presence of NATO land forces in the exposed areas ensures that in the event of a Soviet invasion an immediate collision will occur, thus to all intents and purposes guaranteeing that all members of the Alliance contributing to those forces will automatically be involved regardless of whose territory is actually attacked. At the same time the deployment of conventional forces of sufficient substance to blunt the spearhead of a Soviet invading army, though, admittedly, not to drive it back, provides an opportunity for a 'flexible response' to Soviet attack which may itself be of a purely conventional character in its initial stages. This is to say, that in some circumstances it may be possible for all sides to re-consider their positions and policies before engaging in all out, indiscriminately catastrophic nuclear warfare.

The viability of the North Atlantic Alliance is, of course, conditional on general and continuing confidence in the loyalty of all members, but particularly of those members which possess the nuclear arms on which the ultimate military value of the Alliance depends. Leaving aside the complex and, for present purposes, secondary issue of the French relationship with NATO, it may therefore be seen that everything hinges on the active and continued presence of the American and – if to a lesser degree – the British forces deployed in Western Germany. But it is precisely in this respect of their continued willing-

[9] Cmnd. 2901, 1966.

C

ness to maintain forces there and to employ them in the agreed manner that both the United States and Britain have managed to arouse the suspicions of their allies in recent years. Now that the United States has developed a fully operational system of intercontinental ballistic missiles and is capable, theoretically, of opting out of the European theatre of operations should it wish to do so, the doctrine – indeed, the very possibility – of flexible response has become suspect. American experiments with mass ferrying of troops across the Atlantic have seemed to confirm such fears. In the case of Britain it is principally her insistence on making the presence of the bulk of her troops conditional on the financial assistance of her allies in maintaining them that has aroused doubts about her commitment to NATO. It is not without significance that Britain shares, in reduced form, the two major strategic advantages of the United States – a nuclear capability and a sea barrier to conventional attack – which are the ultimate sources of their allies' concern lest they fail to throw their lot in with the rest at the decisive moment.

But the problem goes beyond such calculations of likely behaviour in the event of Soviet aggression, particularly now that unprovoked Soviet attack appears increasingly improbable – if, indeed, there ever was a serious possibility that the Russians would launch an old-fashioned, armed invasion of western Europe in the manner to which the Germans have accustomed us in this century. There can be little doubt that the withdrawal or even serious diminution of British participation in the NATO landforces would be almost as heavy a blow to the Alliance, though not as immediately dramatic, as a withdrawal by the Americans. With France all but gone from NATO, the Alliance would then appear to rest on an American-German axis and the prospects of eventual American defection following the effective loss of her two principal European allies – Britain and France – would be greatly enhanced. One way or another the calls inside and outside Germany, but particularly inside, to step up her military power and to add nuclear to conventional weapons would greatly increase in intensity and plausibility. The weaker members of the alliance would have to conclude that they must rely increasingly on Germany for their defence – or totally reorient their policy. American amenability to German moves towards re-unification would doubtless increase and within West Germany itself the campaign for unification would not only be intensified but begin to appear a matter of practical politics. At the same time Russian hostility to the rump western Alliance would also increase very greatly. All in all, given that one great and ineradicable source of East-West tension is the division of Germany between the blocs and given that this division is, at the same time, the only readily conceivable issue on which the blocs could be expected to divide to the point of armed conflict, a vast and extremely perilous change in the European scene would be in the making. Everything therefore points to the supreme importance of maintaining the present-day structure and content of the Atlantic Alliance for as long as possible, and to the near certainty that a diminution of the British contribution to NATO would only weaken it and weaken it, moreover, in the particular direction Britain has most reason to fear: a resurgence of Germany as the preponderant power on the Continent and an intensification of those lines of development the convergence of which are most likely to precipitate conflict with the Soviet Union.

It is not surprising, therefore, that there is very little disagreement in Britain today about the desirability of maintaining ground forces in Germany. The question that exercises the Government and informed opinion, however, is whether Britain can afford the economic costs of so doing. Government policy, officially formulated, is to maintain them

'at about their existing level [some 55,000 men] until satisfactory arms control arrangements have been agreed in Europe *provided*, however, that some means is found for meeting the foreign exchange cost of these forces.'[10]

The cost of the British Rhine Army is considerable – about £180 million in 1965/66 of which £85 million was borne in foreign exchange. Of this fully a half was payment on and to personnel, much of it expended by the troops and their families in Germany.[11] Great efforts have been made to reduce this vast addition to Britain's balance of payments problems. Stockpiles have been reduced from what would be required for thirty days' fighting to ten days' supply (chiefly to make possible the dismissal of thousands of local employees) and there has been continual pressure on the Germans to lighten the economic load by making corresponding civil and military purchases in Britain. The reduction of stockpiles has been justified with the argument that it would in any case be absurd to envisage protracted conventional war in central Europe, but it remains a fair question whether this particular egg did or did not precede the chicken. The argument that the Germans should pull their weight rather more

[10] *Defence Review*, 1966. (Italics added.) However, in December, 1967, the NATO Defence Ministers agreed to Britain withdrawing one brigade group (about 6,000 men) provided it continue to be assigned to the NATO order of battle and be returnable to Germany in case of need within ten days.

[11] *Times*, 1 November, 1966.

than they have done until now is equally plausible, but the fact that it is put at all tends somewhat to vitiate the political and psychological foundations of the Alliance. It has the effect of implying that the role of the NATO ground forces is the defence of West Germany, not of the member states collectively in Germany. As the German minister most immediately concerned with the negotiations on offset purchases has put it:

'The troops are there not only for our protection. If the common defence concept of the alliance demands that the troops stay where they are, then the question of whose balance of payments is affected should not arise.

'If the troops are *not* needed for strategic reasons, however, they should be withdrawn, even if the foreign exchange costs were to be offset.'[12]

Meanwhile the difficulty of reconciling the dictates of national defence with those of national economic health remains and continues to pursue the British Government.

The second major example of incompatibility between central goals of British foreign policy is that which obtains between the settled principle of maintaining the closest possible political and military association with the United States and that of entering into a lasting and economically fruitful association with the members of the European Economic Community.

The essential characteristics of Britain's 'special relationship' with the United States are three. Firstly, that it is of very long standing – some historians date it from Britain's mild reaction to President Cleveland's threat in December 1895 to impose a settlement of the Anglo-Venezuelan boundary dispute by war if necessary.[13] Secondly

---

[12] Finance Minister Franz-Josef Strauss, *Times*, 17 March, 1967. Much the same point has been made – from the British angle – by Mr. Enoch Powell, defence spokesman for the Conservative Opposition: 'Our commitments under the North Atlantic Treaty are not conditional, only to be fulfilled if somebody will kindly find a way to relieve us of the cost in foreign currency.' *Times*, 7 November, 1966.

[13] 'This was certainly one of the most unexpected, least warranted, and least excusable steps ever taken in modern times by a Great Power. . . . The message [to Congress] evoked a frenzy of Jingoism throughout the United States; but a chastening influence was exerted by a catastrophic fall in American stocks. British opinion displayed restraint from the start. It became obvious that, while an Anglo-American war would still be the most popular of all wars in America, in England it was viewed as fratricidal.' R. C. K. Ensor, *England, 1870–1914*, Oxford, 1949, p. 230.

that its prime (but not exclusive) value in British eyes has been military. And thirdly, that it has always been an asymmetrical relationship, signifying different things to either side. Indeed, as a political concept the 'special relationship' is largely a British creation which few influential Americans have accepted without serious reservations.

Originally, the establishment of Anglo-American amity as a principal – later the principal – dogma of British foreign policy arose out of the recognition of growing American power at the end of the nineteenth century: conflict with the United States was to be avoided at all costs. But slowly emerging recognition of Britain's own failing powers relative to her potential and actual enemies altered the basis of the dogma. In its present form it rests on the belief that it is vital to British security not merely to avoid conflict with the United States but to have her actively on her side in conflict with third parties. The military isolation of the United Kingdom in 1940, the working Anglo-American alliance against Germany during the Second World War, and the developing conflict with the Soviet Union in the aftermath of the war were all seen in turn as amply demonstrating and successively reinforcing the judgment that a close alliance with the United States was both necessary and possible. And though the formal post-war expression of the alliance was the multi-lateral North Atlantic Treaty, everything possible was done by successive British governments to preserve the bi-lateral, *ad hoc* partnership which had developed so strikingly during the Second World War. Even where British moves have been unaligned with, or contrary to, American policy – as in the decision by the Attlee government in 1948 to go ahead with independent production of nuclear weapons – assertion of independence has frequently been justified on the grounds that it would make for an easier, more equal, more even relationship with the Americans. In the special case of nuclear weapons it undoubtedly did for a time. But the growing disparity of resources (and consequent disparity of needs and policy) between the ever stronger super-power and the steadily declining ex-imperial state has slowly undermined whatever hard and resistant reality the special relationship ever had as a partnership of like-minded states sharing many enemies, some fundamental political purposes, a common language and not insignificant commercial and ethnic ties. Even cooperation in the field of nuclear weapons, carefully maintained on an exclusive, bi-lateral basis outside NATO, has now begun to dwindle in the face of Britain's failure to maintain the pace of development. Indeed, recent reports have it that American attention in these matters is beginning to turn to France. For France, despite very heavy American pressure to desist, has been pursuing nuclear weapons research in the last decade or so with the utmost energy,[14] greater in some respects than Britain.

American interest in cooperation with Britain has been largely pragmatic; dogma and sentiment have been almost entirely on the British side. Immediately after the war Britain was, after the United States, the most powerful state outside the Communist bloc. Large areas of the world could be 'policed' and pre-empted from Soviet and then Chinese influence by Britain. Moreover, Britain possessed and could offer the United States a vast series of bases and *points d'appui* extending from metropolitan Britain herself across the Mediterranean, Africa and the Middle East and into the Indian Ocean to South-east Asia. Over and above her capacity for exerting world-wide influence Britain was the one considerable non-communist state in Europe to have escaped defeat in the war and therefore, and by virtue of her political structure and prestige, the natural cornerstone of any European, anti-Soviet alliance.

The decline of American interest in partnership with Britain stems very largely from the diminution of the latter's military power, the dramatic shrinking of the areas subject to her political influence and the emergence of additional candidates for partnership in all parts of the world among both the defeated states and those newly sovereign. However Britain may have been applauded by Americans – officially and unofficially – as she withdrew from areas which had been under her authority and influence, the net effect upon her partnership with the United States was to reduce its value in American eyes. And if this was not always immediately clear either to the Americans or to the British in the first decade after the war it became obvious – and, indeed, public – as the political evolution of Africa, Asia and Latin America began to assume greater importance for the major powers *pari passu* with the relative crystallization of the situation in Europe. Not unnaturally, therefore, it has been part of Britain's effort to retain her status as a partner not only to cooperate with the United States in the developing world,[15] but to keep up an independent presence in areas which she would otherwise have been inclined to evacuate. This, as has been noted, is notably the case in South-east Asia where the United States has been anxious to see Britain sharing the burden of indirectly containing China – partly to avoid further investment of her own resources, but perhaps chiefly because political circum-

---

[14] See for example: *Times*, 9 December, 1966; 8 March, 1967.
[15] For example in British Guiana where a potentially pro-Soviet government was forced out of power.

stances do not permit the United States to replace Britain with any ease, if at all. By the time the Indonesian 'confrontation' of Malaysia had lapsed the British Government, as has been said, was resolved to pull out of Singapore. It was American pressure to reverse the decision that seems to have caused the Cabinet to hesitate for a time – until the economic crisis at the end of 1967 moved it to set December 1971 as the limiting date.

Whereas the preservation of Britain's relationship with the United States as a cardinal goal of foreign policy has been deeply imbedded in British diplomatic and military thinking for many years, official interest in a closer association with the states of western Europe is of recent vintage. The first formal application to join the European Economic Community was made in 1961 by a Conservative government. Only in 1967 did the leading members of the Labour Party finally and publicly resolve on a similar step, again unsuccessful, but at any rate practically excluding the subject from that time on from the sphere of inter-party, though not *intra*-party, dispute – as the 'special relationship' had always been excluded.

This shift in British policy was chiefly based upon a new, hard look at the nation's economic circumstances – fear of being priced out of a very large and promising market,[16] fear of the consequences of limited size in a technological age which gives untold advantages to those capable of large-scale production based upon a large internal market, and fear of loss of traditional as well as of new extra-European markets in the face of European competition. It was helped along by growing impatience with the Commonwealth and increasing disbelief in it as a source of benefit to its leading member as a latter-day substitute for empire – at one and the same time the means whereby Britain would retain her world-wide role and the justification for doing so.[17]

[16] Between 1958 and 1964 United Kingdom exports to the EEC increased by 97·5%, while exports to the Commonwealth increased by only 1·6%. Imports from the EEC increased by 73·8%, from the Commonwealth by 30·5%.

[17] Thus, the Commonwealth Correspondent of the *Times* (21 February, 1967): 'Disenchantment with the Commonwealth has . . . become marked in the past five years. The reasons are not creditable and not really cogent, but they should be faced. Briefly they seem to be:

  (i) The failure of the new emergent countries in Asia and Africa to retain British political and legal traditions as did Canada and Australia.

 (ii) The embarrassing exposures of Commonwealth impotence by such developments as the Indo-Pakistan war and the behaviour of Dr. Nkrumah.

(iii) So many other failures—like the West Indies federation, and the emergence of petty states claiming equality with India or Canada.

(*continued on next page*)

But interest in the EEC has not implied a total reorientation of British foreign policy. There has been no question (at any rate in Whitehall and Downing Street) of entering the Community as a preliminary to participation in a union of states in which the traditional, jealously protective and competitive, sovereign identities of its members would gradually be displaced by that of a super-state capable of meeting Russia and America on something like equal terms. Nor has there been any serious question of relaxing the effort to maintain the politico-military alignment with the United States, even though some of the weightiest arguments for association with the EEC states are founded on fears of America's *economic* power. This is partly because reluctance to embark on the adventure of disestablishing the structure of national sovereignty is very strong in Britain, possibly stronger than anywhere else in Western Europe; partly because successive British governments have been convinced that only the United States can ensure the security of Europe against Soviet pressure in all the forms that pressure can take; partly because there continues to be a strong sense of ideological and cultural identification with the United States, whereas 'Europe' is still a term which implies a distinction between Britain and the continental states; and finally, because since the accession of General de Gaulle to power in 1958 projects for the political integration of Europe have in any case not been practical politics. In itself, Britain's lack of interest in European integration could provide a strong basis for Franco-British cooperation. But as the complement of Britain's cool approach to the 'European idea' is insistence on the American relationship, the potentiality for Franco-British cooperation has been neutralized by de Gaulle's implacable resistance to all forms of American preponderance in European affairs, including that of influence by proxy through Britain. It may be that there was once a chance of the French reconciling themselves to an Anglo-French diumvirate in an enlarged EEC. If there was, it was killed once and for all by the Nassau agreement between Kennedy and Macmillan in 1962. This, by making Britain's nuclear weapons capability irrevocably dependent on the United States, could be seen as irrefutable evidence of Britain's determination not to go it alone in the French (or Gaullist) manner. However this may be, General de Gaulle ap-

(*continued*)
   (iv) Commonwealth immigration, which brutally showed that the Commonwealth could be really multi-racial only at the official, professional and ministerial levels.
   (v) The peculiar stridency of the African leaders and the unpopular hostilities with the white Rhodesians.
   (vi) The rise in aid, and the (relative) decline in trade.'

pears to have made up his mind that Britain was not a partner he could work with. Accordingly, it was the French who vetoed Britain's entry into the EEC in 1963 and 1967, and who retain the decisive voice in this respect to this day. But what is, for them, the key element of the problem – the nature of Britain's central political and military policy – remains, in British eyes largely irrelevant to the question of her membership in the EEC. And, indeed, there has been barely any wavering on it in London:

'It is sometimes suggested that if Britain is to join the European Economic Community we must change our relations with the United States, particularly over defence, and abandon the role we play in the outside world. To this the Government are resolutely opposed.'[18]

The desire, on economic grounds, to enter the European Economic Community has grown, rather than diminished, since Britain's first application was turned down. Awareness and understanding of the political – i.e. French – obstacles to entry has grown rapidly and to many they appear, at the time of writing, to be insuperable, at any rate in the sense that Britain's entry is now clearly conditional on a fundamental re-orientation of French foreign policy. But, again, up to the time of writing, there has been no hint or evidence of willingness seriously to accommodate French policy or, alternatively, of any move to abandon the project and seek modified economic salvation elsewhere. Britain's treatment of her European Free Trade Area partners has, on occasion, been brutal – as when she instituted a surcharge on all imports in 1964 without even giving them prior notification. Talk of an Atlantic, i.e. US-oriented, free trade area has generally and probably correctly been laughed out of court.

Yet while British loyalty to her own conception of the Anglo-American relationship has remained practically unimpaired throughout the 1960's, the circumstances in which this relationship must function have been changing all the time. As has been seen, Britain is no longer capable of sustaining world-wide influence and the overseas areas in which she retains an autonomous political-military presence are dwindling rapidly. The 'special relationship' itself is thus taking on a somewhat anachronistic flavour *pari passu* with the decline of the value which the United States sets on it. And one result is an element of unreality in some British assessments of the national predicament. Nevertheless, the persistence with which Britain pursues her policy of entry into the EEC suggests that a reversal of priorities is in the

[18] Foreign Secretary George Brown in the House of Commons, 16 November, 1966.

making, i.e. that the manner in which politico-military security is ensured must be accommodated to the dictates of economic strength, rather than the reverse. Ultimately, if the quest is successful, the 'special relationship' may therefore fade away completely. This need not occur, of course, any more than it is inevitable and indispensable, as opposed to desirable and profitable, that Britain enter the EEC. The priority which governments accord to economic interests, however, has been notable throughout most of recent British history and the anxiety to enter the EEC may be seen as reflecting a reassertion of the traditional primacy of economics and finance in Britain over diplomacy and defence – and, up to a point, of the influence of the Treasury and other insitutions of economic and financial administration on the making of foreign policy.[19]

[19] This is not meant to suggest that the Foreign Office has been opposed to entry into the EEC. Quite the contrary. What has happened is that the really effective arguments for entry within the policy-making machine have been economic and these have been particularly effective because they were adopted and advanced by the Treasury. Political arguments for entry have been either of marginal, or no importance. Considerations of where Britain's political and military interests lie, as formulated by the Foreign and Defence establishments, have either remained intact – even where incompatible with considerations of economic interests – or else been slowly and unwillingly, or even unconsciously adjusted to the generally accepted view of the nation's economic requirements and of their primacy. The final acts of major surgery in January 1968 – the decision to withdraw from Singapore and from the Persian Gulf and to scrap plans for an advance air strike capability based on the F111 aircraft – were taken on relatively narrow, but classic Treasury grounds coupled to a surrender to left-wing pressure within the Labour Party. Defence and external policy considerations were, after a struggle, overruled.

III

The Machinery

(I) THE POLICY MAKERS

FOR the reasons suggested the problems of comprehending the external environment of the State, of defining its goals, and of formulating its policy all entail administrative and intellectual challenges of the highest order and the greatest difficulty. The actual business of implementing policy and of attempting to advance, however slowly and erratically, towards a defined political goal is of greater difficulty still. It involves problems which may be incapable of solution even in the abstract. And its success or failure at any given stage will be determined not only by the objective, environmental features of the situation confronting the policy-making machine – such as the strength of its political and material resources as opposed to the countervailing actions of other states – but by the subjective factor of the efficacy of the machine itself as manifested in its efficiency of analysis and execution, the clarity and validity of the goals it sets itself, and the coherence of its approach to the foreign scene as a whole. The process of policy-making may thus be seen as an outcome of the interaction between elements of an outer world in (and on) which the policy-makers are bound to operate and the inner, mental and administrative world of the policy-makers themselves.

It follows from this that as a preliminary to an attempt to set out and analyze the process of foreign policy-making it is essential to identify the group of individuals within the state who are involved in it and to define, if only within fairly loose limits, the locus of their activity within the state administration as a whole. This task, however, is one of extreme complexity. There is no universal solution generally applicable to all countries at all times. Office (e.g. foreign minister and principal functionaries of the ministry of external affairs) is not always a reliable indicator of close involvement in the process, still less is it an unambiguous indicator of what might be termed central or decisive involvement. It is by no means rare for a minister of defence or of finance or for their subordinates to have a greater influence on the evolution of policy than those nominally responsible for it. It is frequently extremely difficult to trace the origins of policy – as opposed to policy-decisions – but it is clear that the germ out of which a fully formulated policy has grown may have been contributed by a distant envoy, or by a member of the legislature, or by a journalist, or an academic. None of these need fall into the category of policy-makers – yet they must all be considered if the process as a whole is to be understood.

Furthermore, effective authority may lie outside the formal machinery of government – as it did in Stalinist Russia – and even where it is firmly within it there may be competing, hostile and parallel hierarchies of command and execution – as in Hitlerite Germany. The extent to which the minds of key individuals will have been made up in all significant respects before attaining political power and access to official sources of information and advice varies enormously from case to case. In brief, one need not be committed to a systematically conspiratorial interpretation of political events to recognize that even in the most orderly and constitutional of states the processes of policy-making, foreign or domestic, spill over into society at large and cannot be understood where examination is limited to the machinery of government alone.

Nevertheless, a fairly clear, nominal distinction can and must be made between those who contribute to the process – junior members of the government, diplomats in foreign posts, senior officers of the armed forces, the lower ranks of the official hierarchy at home, spokesmen for interest groups and lobbies, journalists, and, in a wider sense, the foreign governments concerned through their own official and unofficial spokesmen – and those who have the effective authority and responsibility and take the decisions in each particular case.

In reality, even this distinction will be far from sharp. The locus of the dividing line will vary with the importance attached to the particular question: minor matters being generally settled at a low hierarchical level after relatively limited consultation restricted to a small group, major questions being generally decided at a high level following more careful discussion in a wider circle. And it will vary with contingent factors such as the simultaneous pressure of other government business in hand at the time and with considerations of secrecy. There is, too, the factor of error: junior officials may not perceive the likely implications of their actions and take decisions on their own. Senior officials and political chiefs may fail to consult subordinates. There may be disloyalty: the forum in which a matter is debated may be enlarged or restricted improperly and without warrant. Thus, while it may be possible, in principle, to determine in retrospect to whom the responsibility for a particular decision should be attributed and who, in contrast, may have played no more than a contributory role in the course of the process that culminated in the political decision under review, it would be misconceiving the nature of the process to attempt to class a given individual or function or office as belonging finally and unequivocally to one category rather than the other.

Strictly speaking, this applies to the most important and influential political leaders and posts no less than to the most remote and junior officials. Many decisions are taken at the lower reaches of the official hierarchy on the basis of a purely intuitive conviction that they would be approved of if brought to the attention of the men at the top without any attempt being made to test the belief in practice. Who, in such cases, is the policy-maker – as distinct from contributor to the policy-making process – is a question that comes close to being one of semantics. Nevertheless, if we continue to use the term 'policy' only with reference to those who have the authority or ability to commit the machinery of state and a significant fraction of national resources to the end in view,[1] there is no real difficulty in seeing the official who has the authority or, more rarely the courage to take major decisions without reference to higher authority as falling into one of two categories. He may be actuated by his understanding of the outlook of his masters – in which case it is they, not he, who are the makers of policy in almost all significant respects. Alternatively, he may be actuated by his private outlook in contradistinction to that of his masters, in which case the machinery of policy-making may be said to be in process of breaking down and being replaced by two or more parallel (though not coequal) hierarchies of assessment and execution which may or may not be centrally coordinated. Such fissures may occur at the top : a powerful minister of defence or chief of staff may make both his own assessment of the situation and his own diplomatic dispositions, through the armed services attachés, for example. Or they may occur lower down in the hierarchy, or even in the field : a group of like-minded officials or a particularly strong and stubborn ambassador may attempt to shift their government from its position by pursuing an independently conceived policy in the expectation, say, that a series of *faits accomplis* will suffice to decide the issue.

Divisions of view and assessment, as opposed to differences of policy, within the policy-making and policy-implementing machinery are anything but rare, however, except perhaps in the most dictatorial

[1] Cf. a formal definition of policy, p. 11.

and terrorized of state administrations. How far the various arms of government and administration will in fact coordinate their estimates and actions depends chiefly, other things being equal, on the complexity of the matter at issue. Indeed, and as will be seen, the intricacy of contemporary external affairs is such that even with good-will and loyalty on all sides it is extremely difficult to muster undifferentiated support from all concerned. But just how much good-will there is, how loyal each level in the administrative hierarchy is to the others, and how far private views, interests and ambitions may outweigh constitutional and ideological obligations of loyalty and cooperation will vary enormously from country and to country and from issue to issue. Across the gulf in time, place and situation that separates them, it is worth recalling – and comparing – the so-called Curragh Mutiny of British officers opposed to Irish Home Rule in 1914 with the very real mutiny of French officers in May, 1958, over independence for Algeria.

Disloyalty and unconstitutional practice are factors which cannot be easily assimilated into a study of constitutionally legitimized institutions and processes without very greatly widening its scope. But, fortunately for present purposes, in contemporary British practice the incidence of deviation from the constitutional norm is very low. The influence of the civil service on British policy-making is certainly very powerful, but what chiefly characterizes its relations with the political component of the hierarchy is nevertheless its fundamental and ultimate docility. On the whole, its influence is brought to bear through the machinery itself according to a plan and in a manner well-understood and accepted by all concerned. There have been notable occasions when the political chiefs have ignored the advice of their official advisers (as in the period of the appeasement of Germany before the Second World War) or have carefully avoided consulting them at all (as in the preparations for the Suez Operation). But there has been no known significant case in modern times of the reverse occurring – of officials taking matters into their own hands or of collective stonewalling, or even of concerting resignations on a scale large enough to impress the public or frighten the Government.[2] Nevertheless, such

[2] There were a few resignations after Suez, but not on a scale sufficiently large to alarm the Cabinet. More recently, in February, 1966, the Chief of Naval Staff, Admiral Sir David Luce, asked to be relieved of his post (five months before the date on which he was in any case due to retire) because of his disapproval of the Government's decision to build no more aircraft carriers. His political chief, Mr. Christopher Mayhew, Minister of Defence for the Navy also resigned, but on somewhat different and more complex grounds.

(continued on next page)

possibilities must be borne in mind. Successful constitutional government implies, among other things, a measure of consent and support on the part of all concerned – and all those who believe themselves to be concerned – with the business at hand. Where conviction is lacking, respect for constitutional principles, habit, and self-interest will usually suffice to ensure that the administrative machine keeps together. But there is probably a limit to the violence that can be done to men's beliefs, opinions and self-respect. It is safer for the political leader, however strong and dynamic, to attempt to carry his collegues and principal subordinates with him. And much the same is true, though to a lesser degree, at lower levels of the official hierarchy. The efficacy of the policy-making machine as a whole hinges on the cooperation and mutual confidence that obtains between those who are at the top of the pyramid of authority and responsibility and those at its base upon whom they depend. In Britain both such cooperation and such confidence are to be found to a high degree.

(II) THE SUPREMACY OF THE EXECUTIVE

In law, no less than in fact, the conduct of Britain's foreign affairs, is the peculiar concern and undivided responsibility of the Executive – a Crown prerogative. While it is true that the power of modern Cabinets to control Parliament is very nearly untrammelled in all spheres, the obligation to seek Parliament's formal consent or authority for very many of the most important activities of government remains. Both precendent and statutory law prescribe that parliamentary consent be granted where such matters as taxation, expenditure, the raising of troops, the nationalization or regulation of industry, or, generally where the pattern of the private citizen's life is liable to be affected in any significant or novel way. And where this consent is not obtained the political consequences of such neglect of Parliament may be serious. Only in wartime or other grave and publicly recognized emergencies will recourse be had to executive orders, but even these are normally limited in scope and time; and they are totally out of the question in certain specific spheres such as money matters.

In the realm of foreign affairs, however, the citizen is only impli-

(continued)
The issue had been hotly debated and many senior naval officers were indignant, but so far as can be made out only one relatively senior officer (a Captain, RN) followed the Chief of Staff into retirement for reasons which were expressly linked to government policy. Following the defence cuts announced in January 1968 the Army's Director of Volunteers and Territorials, a Major-General, submitted his resignation. He too was in any case due to retire later in the year.

cated, as a rule, indirectly or by extension. It may be argued of course, that the physical survival of many citizens, perhaps even the majority, is in fact much more closely bound up with such a question as whether Germany shall ultimately acquire nuclear weapons and what the reaction of the Soviet Government in the event might be, than with the question of, say, the efficacy or otherwise of a Selective Employment Tax. Nevertheless, in formal terms, only the latter question is a direct and unique responsibility of the British Government; and while the approach the Government of the day may adopt to the question of Germany's armaments may be discussed in Parliament and elsewhere, it is clearly not a matter which is susceptible to legislation *per se*. Nor, unlike the Executive in the United States, is the Government specificallly enjoined to seek the Legislature's advice and consent. Nor is there a Select Committee of legislators expert either in principle or in fact on foreign topics and entitled to interrogate the Foreign Secretary and his officials on the reasons underlying policy. Only the bare financial arrangements – perhaps the least important aspect of foreign affairs administration – are subject to review by Parliament in general and the Select Committee on Estimates in particular. But even this latter review occurs no more than once every so many years.

No doubt the Government may be questioned in Parliament and its policies criticized. In a general sense foreign policy, like policy in any other sphere, may be said to be determined by the Government subject to parliamentary confidence in it. And of course, in an extreme case – theoretically, at any rate – this confidence may be withdrawn and the Government turned out. In fact, although Parliament exercises some influence on the making of foreign policy[3] this influence is very slight. Above all, Parliament is in no sense a regular participant in the process, either by right or by custom.

Even those matters which are most crucial and which, at first sight, seem the most appropriate subjects for legislative checks on the Executive – the making of war and peace and the making or ratification of treaties – are, in British constitutional law, termed Acts of State and are undoubted and exclusive prerogatives of the Crown.[4] Certainly no modern government will refrain from bringing its intention to make war before Parliament and, latterly, the practice of laying the texts of treaties and other major international documents on the table of the House of Commons has become somewhat more frequent.

[3] Discussed in Chapter IV.
[4] For a detailed discussion of the matter see E. C. S. Wade and G. Godfrey Phillips, *Constitutional Law* (Sixth Edition), London, 1962, Chapt. 20, pp. 249–64.

Nevertheless, since, in the strict sense, neither the making of war nor the making of treaties require legislation, or even Parliament's approval, and there is therefore no equivalent to the 'committee stage' in which Parliament subjects Bills to detailed scrutiny clause by clause, the legislature once again, has only the revolutionary alternative of rejecting government policy *in toto*. In short, the monopoly which is accorded the Executive in the sphere of foreign affairs *de jure* is consistent to a remarkable degree with the general supremacy of the contemporary Executive over Parliament *de facto*.

The making of foreign policy, then, is the business of the Executive and for almost all practical purposes the Executive is unfettered in its exercise of this function. In any attempt to understand the processes of foreign policy-making in Britain attention must therefore, in the first instance, be concentrated on the administrative machinery which is directly concerned with foreign affairs, whether as its major function or as an incidental or even occasional aspect of its duties, its primary sphere of activity lying elsewhere.

Such an analysis pre-supposes a regularity, a pattern. In fact, just as – and partly because – individual problems in foreign policy almost invariably present aspects which are unique, so the manner in which they are 'processed' by the administrative machine is rarely precisely identical in any two given cases, always excepting those matters which are manifestly trivial. It may therefore be argued that, in a very strict sense, no such pattern can be said to exist because there is no absolute regularity of treatment, analysis, decision, execution, and reconsideration. Nevertheless, it can be shown that the various parts of the machine are, at the present time, related to each other in certain general ways and that, again in a general way, problems of a recognizably specific character are apt to be dealt with by stated organs in a stated manner, while those of a different character tend to be dealt with by other organs according to another, but still recognizable scheme. If it is clearly borne in mind that in any given case and at any given stage the common or prevalent pattern or scheme may be disrupted, and that the flexibility and relative indeterminancy of the system are two of its most significant characteristics, there is no apparent reason why one should not attempt to delineate the rough outline of the administrative machine as it appears to be operating today.

Two preliminary distinctions may be conveniently made. The first is between what might be termed the central core or central column of the policy-making machine and its surrounding mantle – between the formal administrative structure extending from the Cabinet down

D

to the lowliest Third Secretary of Embassy on the one hand, and on the other hand the other bodies and officers concerned or involved in external affairs to a greater or lesser extent, but never exclusively and never possessed of equivalent authority at a given hierarchical level – the Monarch, the military, the Treasury, the Board of Trade, the atomic energy establishment, and so forth. The latter's views or departmental policies or interests may, in certain circumstances, be decisive. But these views or policies arise out of considerations which, in the strict sense, do not relate to foreign policy whether the emphasis is on the first term of the phrase or the latter. The Treasury views foreign affairs, perforce, in the light of essentially domestic considerations. The Defence Chiefs are, in an obvious respect, concerned with foreign affairs; but they are not concerned with foreign policy as such, even though their influence over it may, on occasion, be very great.

The second distinction that must be made is between the organs of the Executive proper which participate in the making of foreign policy as of constitutional and institutional right and those bodies or personalities which are not part of the Executive, or necessarily even part of the formal structure of government, but which nevertheless may influence the process because, together, they form the domestic environment in which the foreign policy-makers operate. These range from Parliament with its undoubted – and still living – privilege of requiring the Government to define and justify its policy publicly to the impact a single journalist may have, both through his newspaper and through his contacts, on the formulation of policy. It would be highly misleading to ascribe to Parliament, the Parties, the press, certain semi-academic institutions such as Chatham House, and to the less easily dissected circles of influence that may be loosely grouped under the heading of the London Clubs and the Old Boy Net a central role in the day-to-day processes of foreign policymaking. But to ignore the role of the non-responsible or unofficial institutions and their contribution, particularly in the long term, towards the determination of the climate in which the responsible and official officers of the Executive operate is to miss much that is characteristic of British administrative procedure and of British foreign policy itself.

(III) THE CABINET

At the pinnacle of the British system of government is the Cabinet. It derives its collective authority from the fact that its members are at once leaders of the political party in power, managers of the business of Parliament and, for the most part, chiefs of the major administrative departments. In ultimate terms the Cabinet *is* the Executive. There is nothing of significance in the public domain that is beyond its purview and there is no body or individual within or beyond the Constitution in whom are vested superior powers. In practice, however, the Cabinet is first and foremost a body that deliberates and decides, leaving execution to others, and it does so largely on the basis of the information with which it is supplied by those members of the Government, whether in the Cabinet or not, who are immediately concerned with the issues in question.

Which matters do in fact come before the Cabinet, at what stage, in what circumstances and at whose initiative – are therefore all questions of some importance. Generally, only those of some weight will come before it, but the criteria are never firm. In the modern period the steadily increasing pressure of business has moved the threshold dividing major from minor matters upwards and various devices, most notably that of Cabinet Committees, have been insituted in an attempt to maintain the Cabinet's effective hold on the full range of government business. The threshold itself is flexible in other respects. A strong Minister may be less inclined to consult his colleagues (with the implied obligation of subsequently abiding by their decision) than a weak one. And, as we shall see, the personality, experience and predilections of the Prime Minister of the day and his general views on procedural and constitutional matters are all determinants of the greatest importance – so much so, in fact, that it may be said with some confidence that no two Cabinets operate in quite the same manner and that the differences between the customary procedure of one modern Cabinet and another may be great enough to influence the substance of the business, let alone the form.

Nevertheless, the fundamental and characteristic fact is that once a question has come before the Cabinet and the issue been decided one way or the other, no Prime Minister and certainly no Minister, however resolute or personally influential, will ignore or attempt to circumvent that decision. In this sense the Cabinet is the supreme authority within the Executive machine and its paramountcy within the executive domain is of an absolute and final character – unlike in the legislative and political domains where, for all its overwhelming force, it may yet be questioned and, in principle, overriden.

It follows that the less a Cabinet concerns itself directly and on a day-to-day basis with the affairs of a given department, or the greater its confidence in a certain Minister (which usually comes to the same thing) the freer is the Minister in question to formulate and put into execution a policy which is, in a significant sense, his own. Because foreign affairs are rarely of crucial domestic political importance and because the probability of senior politicians being familiar with them through past ministerial experience is relatively low,[5] it is unlikely that other Cabinet members acquire the same facility in dealing with external problems as their training and duties compel them to acquire in the domestic sphere. They may have strong views on certain broad issues, views which as often as not are formed when in opposition. But for the most part the effect of Cabinet Papers and Cabinet discussions appears to be a sobering one: the complexity and delicacy of questions in foreign policy is soon enough comprehended without a command of their detail ever being acquired by any but the specialist Ministers. These specialist Ministers are therefore, in some respects, in a stronger position in relation to their own fields than the other Ministers in relation to theirs. And the possibility of formulating a foreign policy bearing a personal stamp is correspondingly somewhat greater than in the economic field or that of the social services, provided that foreign policy can, in some sort, be isolated from or made independent of, say, questions in economic policy. Where this cannot be done – as is not infrequently the case – the full effects of Cabinet government are immediately apparent. As soon as a foreign question is susceptible to relation, however tenuous, to domestic matters and accordingly comes within the official purview and expert competence of another department, and its Minister, the full force of the Cabinet system of government is felt. Indeed, if there is a single characteristic of the processes of British foreign policy-making that deserves special emphasis it is the manner and degree to which the handling of foreign affairs is liable to be integrated at the policy-making level with that of all the other business of the nation. This integration is not of equal strength at all times and under all Cabinets. Nor should the fact of integration be taken to mean that foreign and domestic affairs are dealt with in a similar manner and spirit. There are, as will be shown, important differences with quite far-reaching consequences. But the fact remains that, increasingly in the modern period, the traditional and *a priori* distinction between foreign and domestic affairs has been breaking down in Britain – as elsewhere. Policy in one field will be justified in terms of the other in a way which would have struck nineteenth century foreign ministers as odd, even unseemly. Fundamentally, this is probably due to the growing belief,

---

[5] Both Sir Anthony Eden's 1955 Cabinets were exceptional in that over two-fifths of their members (including the Prime Minister) were either directly concerned with external and defence affairs or had served with the Foreign Office in the past.

at least in Western Europe, that the salvation of nations is to be sought in domestic prosperity and welfare rather than international influence and military power and that, in any case, the latter depend, in practice, on the former and must be justified, if at all, in its terms. But in Britain, thanks in part to the powerful Cabinet system whereby all major aspects of national life are discussed by a relatively small, uniquely authoritative group of men, this process has been carried further than in most countries. The political fact today that the Treasury maintains a crucial influence on British foreign and defence policy no doubt follows, to some extent from Britain's national circumstances. But it is the administrative and constitutional structure of the Executive, notably the Cabinet system, which has made the increasing and accelerating subordination of 'foreign' to 'domestic' affairs possible.[6]

It is of the essence of the British system of government and administration that decisions are rarely taken by one man alone, or without all interests being fully represented. In a sense, the Cabinet is the supreme committee[7] in a land where committees are 'an important part of what is referred to with reasonable pride as "the British way of life".'[8]

Such is the norm. Where gross departures from it are made the results are clearly evident.

(IV) PREMIER AND MINISTERS

While the Cabinet – collectively – is supreme, the Prime Minister can and generally does dominate it. It is he who forms it and selects Ministers for particular posts and, subject to party-political circumstances, they continue to occupy them only so long as he desires them to do so. His function as party leader in the television age confirms and enhances a public position, and corresponding political prestige, that none of his colleagues can possibly rival. Through his control of Cabinet business, the Cabinet Secretariat, the Security Services and official patronage he is personally in possession of administrative instruments of great force. Finally, his own, direct contribution to the management of foreign relations and the making of foreign policy at the highest level is such that within the field of external affairs as a whole his is probably by far the most powerful single office.

[6] Along with Treasury control of government expenditure. But see Chapter IV on the possibility of drawing a valid distinction between 'foreign' and 'domestic'.

[7] Though not in the technical meaning of the term as the Cabinet is clearly not subordinate to a higher body to which it is responsible. Cf. K. C. Wheare, *Government by Committee*, Oxford, 1955, p. 6.

[8] *Ibid.* p. 1.

In the first place, there is no question today of what might be termed unilateral management of foreign relations by the Foreign Secretary – in the manner familiarly illustrated by Palmerston under Lord John Russell in the middle of the last century – even subject, as ultimately Palmerston was too, to ultimate Cabinet authority. True, in our own day a British Prime Minister may, in principle, resolve on abdicating his overriding responsibility in favour of his Foreign Secretary. The last to do so to any significant degree was Baldwin, thirty years ago; but even then the abdication was not complete. None of his successors followed his example and it would be surprising if any did so in the future. Over and above the Prime Minister's chairmanship of the Cabinet and consequent overview of all government business, the personal participation of heads of government in major diplomatic confrontations has become a regular and predictable feature of international relations.

Diplomatic customs tend to be tenacious and irreversible because departure from them may be thought to require political interpretation. In consequence, such practices as ambassadorial meetings with prime ministers, the participation of prime ministers and their equivalents at summit conferences, and regular visits to major capitals by the heads of states of all sizes to meet their homologues in the major countries are all unlikely to disappear or diminish in frequency in the foreseeable future. Above all, if the basic purpose of serious diplomacy is to influence, it is unlikely that attempts by foreign diplomats to deal with the most influential personality *ex hypothesi* within a given governmental system will cease. The Prime Minister is, and is likely to remain, a super-Foreign Secretary.

Secondly, it is the Prime Minister who determines not only who will be Foreign Secretary in his Government, but what his role will be, how free he will be in the exercise of his judgment and his official functions, and how closely he, the Prime Minister, will be associated in the consideration of daily problems. Here the past experience and political and personal qualities of the men in question will count for a great deal. When Clement Attlee chose Bevin in 1945 he was well aware that Bevin was a man who 'knew his own mind'[9] and was, moreover, one of the most (if not *the* most) powerful, influential and popular leaders of the newly-victorious Labour Party. There could be little doubt that Bevin would attempt to think Britain's foreign relations out for himself, as he did in the event, and pursue a policy that accorded with his findings. Attlee himself, on the other hand, seems to have been more than content with the arrangement whereby

[9] C. R. Attlee, *As it Happened*, London, 1954, p. 170.

Bevin was in daily control of events, subject to friendly discussion of points of major importance. Attlee's principal pre-occupations were in the domestic realm and this accorded well with his own political background and with a pattern of evolution that was usual until quite recently, namely that Prime Ministers are leaders whose main activity and development have tended to be in the field of internal affairs. It is more than a coincidence that not one of the ten Prime Ministers between Lord Salisbury (1895–1902) and Sir Anthony Eden (1955–57) had been a Foreign Secretary prior to his Premiership.[10]

In great contrast to Mr Attlee's Premiership, Sir Anthony Eden's was distinguished by the fact that he exercised full and constant control over foreign affairs to a degree which has had no parallel since the war.[11] Most observers have seen this as arising out of Eden's very great experience and seniority in foreign relations, easily rivalling that of the permanent officials, and his evident inability to refrain from attempting to direct affairs in a field where he had strong views – and feelings.

But even Bevin, in many ways the most formidable Foreign Secretary Britain has had since Lord Salisbury occupied the office, was careful to take no major decisions without consulting his Prime Minister. It is entirely characteristic that when Secretary Marshall's Harvard speech in June, 1947 had 'roused him to quick and resolute action'

'He hurried across to 10 Downing Street, saw Attlee and told him of the immediate action he proposed to take. Back at the Foreign Office he drafted an urgent telegram to Washington instructing the Ambassador, Lord Inverchapel, to see the Secretary of State at once, express Britain's deep appreciation of the offer contained in the Harvard speech and inform him that Bevin was immediately consulting with the French Foreign Minister and others to see how his offer could best be implemented, and would communicate the results. He then telephoned Paris to acquaint the French Foreign Minister of what he had done and ask for his co-operation. By noon that day the first steps had been taken that led to the formation of the sixteen-nation Organization for European Economic Recovery and the vast and historically decisive plan for Marshall Aid to Europe.'[12]

[10] But Ramsay MacDonald did assume the office of Foreign Secretary along with that of Prime Minister in 1924.

[11] And is only comparable with the case of Neville Chamberlain in the present century.

[12] Francis Williams, *Ernest Bevin*, London, 1952, p. 265.

The relationship between the Prime Minister and the Foreign Secretary is crucial for the conduct of foreign affairs in a third respect. The speed with which affairs evolve in the international arena leads to a corresponding need to take important decisions very rapidly. It is not always possible to convene the full Cabinet at brief notice, nor is it always fruitful to do so even when it is technically possible. It is normal for two full days to elapse between the circulation of the Cabinet papers which permit the Ministers to digest the elements of the problems they will be discussing and the assembly of the Cabinet itself. This is a reasonable procedure and serves to emphasize the difficulty that men who are only superficially familiar with important problems are nevertheless expected to deliberate upon them. Consultation with the Prime Minister thus comes to be – for all Ministers, but particularly for the Foreign Secretary – a partial substitute for discussion in full Cabinet.

Intermediate between the two possibilities of discussion in the full Cabinet and consultation with the Premier alone is the consideration of the problem in a Cabinet Committee. This may either be a permanent Committee of the Cabinet or else an *ad hoc* group of Ministers set up to deal with a specific problem. Such *ad hoc* committees, expected to provide a constant flow of decisions and re-formulations of policy, were constituted, for example, when preparations were being made for the invasion of Egypt in 1956 and ten years later for the purpose of dealing with the Rhodesian problem. The power of the Prime Minister to determine who shall belong to a Cabinet committee – which may amount to an Inner Cabinet – is not the least of his prerogatives. It is always possible to weight the membership and arrive at decisions in the name of the Cabinet that the full Cabinet might not endorse so readily were the problem set before it in detail at an earlier stage.

Finally, the Foreign Secretary is not the only head of department with responsibility for aspects of Britain's external affairs. Directly and exclusively concerned with some sector of the field are the Commonwealth Secretary and the Minister for Overseas Development. Until 1966 there was also a Colonial Secretary; and from time to time other ministers with specially defined responsibilities in the external sphere are appointed. In the Macmillan Cabinet there were for various periods a Minister responsible for Central African Affairs and another for negotiations with the Common Market, both with seats in the Cabinet.[13] So quite apart from the general problem of inter-

[13] The latter (Mr. Heath) was in fact subordinate to the Foreign Secretary, but this may be seen as being outweighed somewhat by his seat in the Cabinet.

departmental coordination where the spheres of two Ministries over-lap – as Defence and Foreign Affairs clearly do – the Prime Minister can, within certain limits, exercise a remarkable degree of flexibility in deciding which Minister will handle or supervise which problem, even where portfolios are not formally or overtly re-distributed.[14]

(V) INTERDEPARTMENTAL COORDINATION

If 'peace is indivisible' public administration is hardly less so. There are few subjects – apart from the merely trivial – which can be treated in absolute isolation from others and there are few questions of policy which do not cut across the nominal or traditional lines of demarcation which separate the fields of responsibility over which Ministers and their specialist civil servants preside. The never ending process of creation and dismantling of Ministries (e.g. Civil Aviation, Technology and Economic Affairs) reflects the practical difficulties in the way of giving a Minister and his staff a reasonably clear field to deal with and a reasonably well defined set of responsibilities. Where the field is too great or too broad to compass handily, command of the substance and detail of the subject, particularly at the highest level, is likely to be weak. Where it is too narrow, the problem of overlapping spheres of activity and conflicting departmental outlooks may hamper progress and shift the balance of attention and energy away from the meat of the matter and on to its handling. The fundamental common denominator for all government business, and therefore for all government departments, is that of material resources; an allocation of financial and material resources for the building of motorways is in ultimate conflict with one for submarines and both requirements conflict with those of the welfare services. In consequence, the most important single instrument of inter-Ministerial co-ordination is the annual national budget and the continuing, day-to-day process of supervision of expenditure (and plans for expenditure) known as Treasury Control.[15] Indeed, the influence of the Treasury on all branches of the administration can hardly be understated and although the impact of its thinking and paramountcy at both Cabinet and departmental levels is most dramatic and best known in the

---

[14] On the general problem of inter-departmental coordination and reconciliation, see below.

[15] For two useful discussions of Treasury Control see: Sir John Woods, 'Treasury Control', *Political Quarterly*, xxv, 4, pp. 370–81; and Samuel H. Beer, 'Treasury Control: the coordination of financial policy in Great Britain', *American Political Science Review*, xlix, 1, pp. 144–60.

domestic context, the long-term effects of the perennial attempt to re-
concile external policy with economic resources are quite as profound. In the functional analysis of the 1963/64 Estimates[16] expenditure in 'Support of External Policy' is divided into Defence (£1,904 m.)
and External Relations (£220 m.). 'External Relations' covers expenditure on aid, information, subscriptions to international organizations
and the administration of the Foreign, Commonwealth and (Board of
Trade controlled) Trade Commission Services.[17] The total figure of
£2,124 m. represents about a quarter of the national budget for the
year in question and is therefore easily the largest category within it.
It is therefore hardly surprising that the problem of resources is one
of the most intractable of those which face contemporary makers of
foreign policy and is a permanent part of the material and political
landscape in which they are obliged to function.

More complex, though not necessarily more difficult to solve, are
the problems of coordination which arise out of the fact that no single
Ministry and *a fortiori* no single Minister is in charge of Britain's external affairs. In the veritable welter of overlapping jurisdictions two
broad classes of divides may be distinguished:

  (a) Between the Departments wholly or predominantly concerned
      with external affairs – that is, between the Foreign Office, the
      Commonwealth Office, the Ministry of Overseas Development
      and the Security Services.[18]

  (b) Between the Departments listed under (a) above on the one
      hand and those Departments that are only partly or marginally
      concerned with external affairs on the other.[19]

There are, thus, three broad spheres where the making of foreign
policy requires inter-departmental coordination:

  (a) in respect of the share of national resources that is to be al-
      located to the support of external policy, and, conversely, in
      respect of the role the instruments of external policy (the Dip-
      lomatic and Armed Services and the overseas aid programme)

---

[16] Cmnd. 1965, Table II.

[17] Since amalgamated into a single Diplomatic Service.

[18] The Colonial Office was absorbed into the Commonwealth Office in August
1966. A Minister personally responsible for Colonial Affairs remained in office
until the end of that year.

[19] In a narrow sense there is hardly any Department which is without an
interest in some internal question or on whose business international affairs
does not impinge at all. Even the Ministry of Social Security, concerned as it
is with the individual inhabitants of the United Kingdom, has reciprocal
arrangements with equivalent organizations in other countries to facilitate its
catering for migrants, temporary residents and the like.

are to play in the general effort to maximize national resources, welfare and security;

(b) where questions of external and domestic policy are conceived by specialist Ministries of either group conflict or require co-operation for their implementation;

(c) where the policies and activities of the four Departments with direct responsibilty for external affairs require adjustment and coordination because of the essential indivisibility of external affairs and the consequent overlapping of jurisdictional lines of demarcation and responsibility.

The first sphere (allocation of resources) is the one where the substance of the questions to be dealt with is the most difficult and, at the same time, having regard to foreign policy-making as a whole, the most fundamental. The questions that arise are generally questions of principle and broad approach, rather than of detail. Their administrative treatment is therefore likely to be relatively simple in that once the issues have been clearly formulated at the departmental level the decision-making must generally be at Cabinet level. But the problems are too numerous and intricate for all to be dealt with by the full Cabinet and much of the business is in practice relegated to a committee of Ministers assisted by a parallel committee of permanent officials with the same departmental distribution. The precise membership is a shifting one, determined, as we have seen, by the Prime Minister.

The formal title of the Cabinet committee concerned with foreign policy is the Defence and Overseas Policy Committee. It evolved from the Defence Committee of the first post-war Labour Cabinet which evolved, in turn, from the War Cabinet or, more properly, perhaps, from the pre-war Committee of Imperial Defence. The White Paper which envisaged its establishment argued in admirably succint terms that

'major questions of defence policy cannot be discussed in purely military terms; they also need to be examined in relation to foreign and economic policy, and in this wider context they often raise further issues which have a considerable political content. Conversely, our political relations with other members of the Commonwealth and with foreign countries bear directly on our defence policy; and the requirements of the Government's financial and economic policies equally affect the size, disposition, and equipment of the Services.'[20]

[20] *Central Organisation for Defence*, Cmnd. 2097, 1963, p. 2.

In Mr Attlee's Government the Prime Minister himself presided over the Defence Committee, whose other members included the Foreign Secretary, the Chancellor of the Exchequer, the Minister of Defence and the Service Ministers, the Minister of Labour and National Service and the Minister of Supply.[21] The composition of the contemporary Defence and Overseas Policy Committee is not publicly known, any more than that of other Cabinet committees. However, the 1963 White Paper laid down that

'These broad issues engage the collective responsibility of Ministers. Subject to the supreme authority of the Prime Minister and the Cabinet, they will be dealt with by [the Committee] which will meet under the chairmanship of the Prime Minister and will normally include the First Secretary of State, the Foreign Secretary, the Chancellor of the Exchequer or the Chief Secretary to the Treasury, the Home Secretary, the Secretary of State for Commonwealth Relations and the Colonies, and the Secretary of State for Defence. Other Ministers will be invited to be present as necessary. The Chief of the Defence Staff and the Chiefs of Staff will be in attendance as the nature of the business requires. Other officials, such as Permanent Under-secretaries or the Chief Scientific Adviser to the Secretary of State for Defence, will also attend as required. The Committee will be supported by a committee of senior officials.'[22]

And it was reliably reported[23] that at a meeting on 8 December, 1967 to discuss the question of selling arms to South Africa the following were present: the Prime Minister, the Foreign Secretary, the First Secretary of State, the Chancellor of the Exchequer, the Lord President of the Council, the Defence Secretary, the Commonwealth Secretary, the Lord Chancellor, the President of the Board of Trade, the Lord Privy Seal, the Minister of Power, the Minister without Portfolio responsible for Security affairs, and the Solicitor General. The Chiefs of Staff were 'called in'. Whether all of these sit on the Defence Committee permanently is doubtful; but most clearly do.

The particular issue of arms sales to South Africa was in fact a classic case of inter-departmental conflict overshadowed, complicated and intensified by inter- and intra-party strife. On purely economic and military grounds there were clear arguments for selling South Africa arms for external defence, if not for internal policing. The loss

---

[21] Herbert Morrison, *Government and Parliament*, London, 1954, pp. 19–20.
[22] The parallel and subordinate committee of officials is presided over by the Cabinet Secretary.
[23] *Times*, 16 December, 1967.

of the South African market would be a heavy blow to Britain's balance of payments and to her arms industry; the prospective loss of naval facilities at Simonstown should the South Africans choose to retaliate would, following the closure of the Suez Canal in the June 1967 Middle East war, jeopardize Britain's remaining military positions in the Persian Gulf and the Far East. In contrast, the arguments for maintaining the ban were put largely in terms of principle and Britain's moral standing in the Afro-Asian world, and not so much by the Foreign Secretary, who was notably in favour of relaxing it, as by the leaders of left-wing opinion in the Cabinet and in the Labour party as a whole. And these, perhaps not entirely coincidentally, included ministers whose own departmental responsibilities were overwhelmingly domestic and could therefore afford to take a calmer view of the consequences of the decision to maintain the ban than, say, the Secretary of Defence.

But on a more profound level the issue was not simply one of the political, economic and ethical aspects of the immediate question whether to sell arms to South Africa. It cut deeply into the much more fundamental questions of Britain's role in the extra-European world, into the costs of that role, into the question whether the exigencies of defence policy should determine economic policy or *vice versa*, and even, by extension and because some Labour Party leaders wanted it that way, how social security in the United Kingdom should be structured. Quite clearly a matter of this importance and of such vast ramifications could only be dealt with by Ministers and among themselves, i.e. at the level of the Cabinet or in its key committee.

In the second sphere of interdepartmental conflict and cooperation (between specialist ministries) an immense variety of business is involved and a very broad range of methods of achieving coordination is practiced. For example, immigration policy is explicitly the joint province of the Home Office and the Ministry of Labour.[24] When the Foreign and Commonwealth Offices issue visas and other entry permits they are in fact acting for the Home Office and Labour Ministry on a contractual basis, so to speak. On the other hand the practical working out of this policy, e.g. the denial of visas to certain travellers and the severe treatment occasionally accorded Commonwealth citizens and aliens on arrival at British ports, can cause considerable em-

[24] Simplifying somewhat, aliens in the full sense require visas, while non-United Kingdom Commonwealth Citizens require either Entry Permits or Employment Vouchers. The latter category is issued by the Ministry of Labour, the former is authorized by the Home Office.

barrassment to Embassies and High Commissions overseas. Pressure for change in the regulations or in the law itself can build up abroad and, in the event, an interdepartmental conflict of interests will soon be in the making. At the level of individual, concrete cases such questions may be settled by the officials concerned – within the scope permitted by the law. But where this cannot be done, because of disagreement, or where the law itself is in question, the search for a solution compatible with the needs of all departments must either be abandoned or sent to a higher level in the hierarchy.

The techniques of co-ordination are extremely flexible. Depending on circumstances, any means of interdepartmental adjustment from an informal telephone conversation between officials who know each other personally to a full dress Cabinet discussion may be invoked. Where a certain class of problems crops up at regular intervals the classic solution is the formally established interdepartmental committee of officials. And this, in turn, may be *ad hoc* or permanent; and when permanent – such as the official committee on economic policy – usually at the Deputy Under-secretary level.

In the last analysis it is the individual official who is judge of whether he can deal with the matter himself. And in making his decision he will, above all, have to consider whether he will not be asked, at some stage, if he has checked with another ministry. His own Minister will have to have the cooperation or acquiescence of the other Minister or Ministers who might regard themselves as being concerned. Thus, ultimately, the impulsion to coordinate and the sanctions in case of failure to do so are functions of the system of the collective responsibility of the Cabinet. It is clear that the Foreign Office could not go ahead with the negotiation of a commercial agreement without consulting and coordinating with the Board of Trade. But it is less clear whether the Board of Trade, as such, can influence the Foreign Office on the political aspects of commercial relations. There is a sense in which everyone can have, and is prepared to express, views on foreign political affairs; but unless they are based on specialized knowledge the views of Board of Trade officials are unlikely to cut much ice with their opposite numbers in the Foreign Office. In contrast, the views of their Minister (i.e. the President of the Board of Trade) will have to be taken into account because ministers are responsible collectively for foreign as for all other classes of policy.

Interdepartmental correspondence and discussion are, however, not the only ways in which international business which is of direct concern to home departments is coordinated. Where negotiation with foreign or Commonwealth governments is envisaged or involved it is the Diplomatic Service which is normally responsible. However, a Minister or official of the Home Civil Service may be specifically delegated for the purpose – in which case he will generally be briefed and accompanied by Diplomatic Service officers. Either way an Ambassador or High Commissioner, acting on a brief prepared by the Foreign or Commonwealth Office will be playing a key role in that it is he who is in principle best placed to advise on how the negotiation should be conducted. But precisely to what degree the roles of the Foreign/Commonwealth Offices and Ambassador/High Commissioner will be determinate at the level of either policy-making or execution will depend on the subject of negotiation. Where negotiations concern a subject which is not essentially political the Head of Mission will be instructed by an inter-departmental committee on which the Foreign or Commonwealth Office are, of course, represented, but whose chairman and secretary will generally be drawn from the Treasury, Board of Trade or whatever other Department is principally concerned. And since in such cases the Ambassador or High Commissioner is in many cases unlikely to be fully master of the subject, his specialist Attaché or Secretary or Counsellor – if he has one – will come into the picture too. Where there is none and if the business justifies it, a specialist may be sent out for the purpose from London. Indeed, the complexity of Britain's foreign relations today are such that large Missions generally include specialists in a very wide variety of topics over and above the traditionally sanctioned and differentiated Naval, Military, Air, Commercial and Information attachés.[25] In fact, a large Mission (most notably the Embassy in Washington) is in some respects a scaled-down version of Whitehall. The notion enshrined in the post-war Eden-Bevin reforms of the Foreign Service[26] that the good, generalist diplomat should be able to turn his hand to most things has suffered a decline, at any rate where matters of high complexity and importance are concerned. It is the specialist who must handle financial negotiations or represent Britain on certain technical international bodies or maintain effective contact with, say, foreign scientific circles and authorities. Conversely, only the specialist is in a position to collect and transmit detailed and reliable information about such topics. In

[25] The Plowden Report (*Report of the Committee on Representational Services Overseas*, Cmnd. 2276, 1964) mentions (p. 92) the following: Labour, Civil Air, Scientific, Atomic Energy, Supply, Agricultural, Veterinary, Petroleum, Shipping, Colonial, Financial, Pensions, Defence Research and Cultural Attachés and Advisers.

[26] Outlined in Cmnd. 6420, 1943.

brief, the system which has traditionally obtained in the military field, where serving officers are specially detailed for temporary attaché duties abroad and constitute the principal link through which regular and official contacts between the armed forces of friendly states are channelled, has spread very widely.

These specialist attachés, once they have taken up their posts abroad, are under the orders of their Head of Mission. But they have the right to correspond directly with their home departments on matters of a non-political character, which is to say, in practice, on matters in their own domain. There is thus ample room for an alignment and coordination of political and technical views in the field, i.e. within the Mission itself and before matters have been put to London. It is at this preliminary stage, if ever, that the formulation of the problem in terms which comprehend more than one viewpoint can be speedily and smoothly effected. This is an extremely precious possibility, even if it is not always exploited.

Coordination of policy and activity in the third sphere (between the four departments and the other services specifically and wholly concerned with some aspect of external affairs) is in many ways the most intricate of all.

At the technical level the techniques of coordination are much the same and the sanction for failure to coordinate is identical. The Ministry of Defence, for example, is responsible for the only firm and regular statement of government policy in the external field as a whole – the Defence Review. Accordingly, it is the Ministry of Defence officials who prepare the first draft of the Review and circulate it – first and foremost to the Foreign and Commonwealth Offices – for comment. And it is worth noting that the drafting of the Review is the responsibility of the civilian defence officials. It is they, not the military, whose business it is to consider the political implications of defence problems and who are accustomed to taking things up with their opposite numbers at the Foreign Office. But all this operates relatively smoothly. The major problems of coordination lie elsewhere.

All governments face the problem of distinct ministries operating within a single field, producing distinct and sometimes conflicting analyses and plans, manned by officers with separate departmental loyalties and career structures and headed by political chiefs who compete with each other for advancement, for the public eye and, last but not necessarily least, compete for the public interest as they comprehend it. But while the first category of departmental divides is common to all states, the second has, in the division of labour between the Foreign and Commonwealth Offices an aspect which is peculiar to the British Executive.

In its origins this division was at once a solution to the constitutional and sentimental difficulties in the way of classing citizens of the 'White' Commonwealth with aliens in the normal usage of the term and part of the deliberate, ideologically oriented and by no means unimaginative movement to replace the waning Empire with an association of states under Britain's leadership. But today, in the words of the 1964 Plowden Report:

'the division of the world for representational purposes into Commonwealth and non-Commonwealth countries impedes the development and execution of a coherent foreign policy. It cuts across every other kind of international grouping and association. Membership of the Commonwealth is only one of the factors which helps to shape the policy of any Commonwealth country and it is rarely the decisive one.'[27]

The Plowden Committee believed that the 'logic of events points towards the amalgamation of the Commonwealth Relations Office and the Foreign Office' but saw this only as an 'ultimate aim'. Fearing that 'to take such a fundamental step now could be misinterpreted as implying a loss of interest in the Commonwealth partnership' they limited their recommendation in this respect to one for a unified Service.[28] A single Diplomatic Service was duly set up on January 1, 1965 from which the separate Foreign and Commonwealth Relations Offices, each under their own Secretary of State, now draw their permanent officials both for service in Whitehall and overseas.

In some spheres the systematic coordination of 'foreign' and 'Commonwealth' activities has gone further. Joint information departments have been set up and a joint political department was established to deal with the specific problem of the Indonesian 'confrontation' of Malaysia. The fact that both ministries are housed under one roof helps. But the major political departments and the economic departments remain distinct and there are sufficient people in the Commonwealth Office who object to a total merger with the Foreign Office (because they suspect that it would be the final blow to the whole Commonwealth idea) to make further progress in the near future uncertain. The system is undeniably an awkward one and where the effort to harmonize British policy towards Commonwealth and non-Com-

[27] Plowden Report, p. 12.
[28] Plowden Report, p. 13.

E

monwealth countries succeeds, 'it succeeds in spite of the system and involves much duplication and expenditure of time and effort.'[29]*

A further problem of coordination between departments wholly concerned with external affairs is of still more recent vintage. Until 1961 economic and technical aid to underdeveloped countries had been distributed either through the Colonial Office or the Commonwealth Relations Office or the Foreign Office – according to the formal status of the country or territory concerned. In 1961 the management of the aid scheme (except for capital projects) was concentrated in a single Department of Technical Cooperation under a Minister of State. But it was clearly proclaimed that the Colonial, Commonwealth and Foreign Secretaries would continue to 'be responsible for matters of general policy',[30] i.e. for laying down the political guidelines. In October 1964 the new Labour Government established a full Ministry of Overseas Development under a political chief of higher rank with a seat in the Cabinet.[31] But responsibility for 'general policy' has remained vested in the Commonwealth and Foreign Offices as before. To what extent the political departments resolutely attempt to harness the programme to Britain's political needs as they understand them cannot be clearly known at this stage. A great deal depends on how cold-bloodedly the Government intends the aid programme itself to be administered. But it would be surprising if the officials of the MOD did not acquire in the course of time, and as a function of their growing and accumulated experience in the field, an outlook which differed in significant respects from those of their colleagues in the Diplomatic Service. The essential point is that administratively distinct sets of officials and ministers have their attention concentrated on aspects of third countries which cannot be effectively separated on the ground. The Government of an East African state does not distinguish in its own mind between political and economic relations with Britain: it rightly sees these as being intimately and functionally related one to the other. Whatever weighty administrative and, indeed, ethical and ideological reasons there may be for making a distinction on the British side between aid and politics, it will be of little interest abroad and may be distrusted. This extremely complex – perhaps barely soluble – problem of coordination has been built into the White-

[29] *Ibid.*, p. 12.

[30] *Times*, 22 March, 1961.

[31] The present Minister for Overseas Development (January 1968) is outside the Cabinet.

*Since this passage was written it has been announced that the Commonwealth and Foreign Office are, finally, to be amalgamated – probably by the end of 1968.

hall system simply by the creation of an independent ministry to deal with a specific category of external affairs.

The third major problem of coordination, that between the military and political sides of the country's external affairs machinery, has the same kind of logic, but is vastly more intricate, very deeply rooted (as it is in almost all countries, of course) and carries with it much graver consequences both for the smooth functioning of the machinery itself and for the welfare and security of the state.

The organizational arrangements devised to make a coordinated defence and foreign policy and – hardly less important – coordinated implementation of that policy possible are of long standing. They range back in time to the Committee of Imperial Defence (now transmuted, as has been said, into the Defence and Overseas Policy Committee of the Cabinet) set up in 1904.

Vertically, they are found at almost every functional level from the Cabinet downwards, notably including the Joint Intelligence and Joint Planning sub-committees of the Chiefs of Staff on which the Foreign Office is represented by senior officials along with officers of the Armed Services. Horizontally, coordination is maintained through the Service attachés[32] who are found in all the principal Missions, the parallel diplomatic and military missions in certain Treaty Organizations, e.g. NATO and CENTO, and the Diplomatic Service officers who serve as political advisers to the regional military commanders overseas. Once again, much can be done semi-informally – on the telephone, over lunch and in 'demi-official' correspondence. And some informal contacts are deliberately built in to the formal structure. For example: officers of the Diplomatic Service form a small but regular part of the annual intake into the Imperial Defence College.

The heart of the twin problems of coordination of activities and of the formulation of an integrated foreign policy which is adequately grounded on, and composed of, political and military elements lies in the fact that diplomats and soldiers necessarily look at much the same material through different sets of lenses equipped with very different filters. They analyse the problems that confront them on the basis of dissimilar selections of evidence, differently weighted for political, economic and military data, judged by different, though not necessarily incompatible criteria. For example, a good military analyst necessarily concerns himself more with capabilities than with intentions, certainly where long-term prospects are in question. But intentions and purposes are precisely what the diplomat is bound to assess,

[32] Termed 'Service advisers' in the High Commissions which represent Britain diplomatically in Commonwealth countries.

sometimes even to the extent of disregarding what appear to be capabilities. The military can formulate both their own position and that of the opponent in reasonably clear and unambiguous terms, resting their case on the relatively hard facts of manpower, armaments, topography, climate, logistic facilities, technology and economic resources. The diplomat cannot; and where he attempts to produce an analysis or recommendation which fails to allow for the inevitable tenuousness of his kind of evidence, for the infirmity of human purpose, and for the unexpected he is rightly suspect. Furthermore the military and civil establishments, taking the latter as a whole, are each large and individually self-contained, each with its professional ethos, its peculiar systems and habits of discipline and authority, its easily differentiated patterns of ambition and status-seeking, and its accumulated conventional wisdom. In these circumstances coordination and adjustment often amount to no more than formal recognition of the other side's expertise and professional authority within its own defined sphere and a continuing attempt to mesh together policy-proposals which derive from different intellectual disciplines operating on dissimilar collations of data.

The 1963 White Paper on defence organization[33] envisaged a Committee in the Cabinet Office which would help to keep the 'military plans of Defence in line with the planning of the overseas and economic Departments'. And that appears to be about as far as it is possible to go at the present time. Even so, the Plowden Committee thought it important to warn against the committee becoming 'a forum where Departments arrive, with the help of a neutral chairman, at the highest common factor of inter-departmental agreement and no more.'[34]

Thus both much of the day to day resolution of inter-departmental disagreement and the fundamental business of adjusting external policy in its political aspect to the country's military capabilities and organization – and vice-versa – tend to be left to the political chiefs and ultimately to the Cabinet.

The general effect of the circumstance that separate authorities exist to deal with the same broad sector of the country's affairs is, naturally enough, to intensify the difficulties that are inherent in all foreign policy-making, no matter how efficient and rational the available administrative set-up may be.[35] Thus three Departments of State played a major role, and a fourth played a minor one, in Britain's handling of the readily identifiable single, albeit highly ramified, prob-

[33] Cmnd. 2097.
[34] *Op. cit*, p. 58.
[35] See Chapter One.

lem of Palestine in 1946–48. The Colonial Office was responsible for the civil authority on the spot, the War Office for the military effort in aid of the civil power, the Foreign Office for the extremely complex international implications of the Palestine problem, and the Admiralty for the physical interdiction of Palestine to Jewish immigrants. So although it was the Foreign Office, through Ernest Bevin, that ultimately determined high policy, the Prime Minister had to be called in from time to time to knock heads together. In practice this meant adopting the views of one party, somewhat modified by regard for the views of the other.[36]

The knocking of heads together may not suffice. Because of the conflicting responsibilities and incompatible views of the Colonial and Commonwealth Relations Offices and their respective Ministers on the future of the component parts of British Central Africa responsibility for the entire region was shifted in March 1962 to a specially created Central African Office under a third Cabinet Minister, R. A. Butler, who continued to serve concurrently as Home Secretary. The Prime Minister of the day, Harold Macmillan, explained to Parliament that it was not 'practicable to secure the desired unification of ministerial responsibility by transferring the functions of either [Minister] to the other.[37] Nevertheless, three months later, in July, a single Minister was put in charge of both the Colonial Office and the Commonwealth Relations Office. The Departments themselves retained their separate existence for the time being. Mr Butler continued as Minister in charge of Central African Affairs until October 1963, when the Secretary for Commonwealth Relations and the Colonies took over the new department as well. The three Departments continued their separate existence under a single Minister until April 1964. The Central African Office was then re-absorbed into the CRO. The final permutation came in August 1966 when the Colonial Office too was absorbed into the re-named Commonwealth Office.

For all these reasons it will again be apparent that the importance of the cabinet as the major forum for the discussion of policy on complex issues – and particularly issues which clearly cut across departmental lines – can hardly be exaggerated. There is provision for certain technical means of facilitating Cabinet discussions – indeed, of making them possible. The Foreign Secretary presents a weekly review of events and Cabinet Ministers receive a daily selection of the more important Foreign and Commonwealth Offices papers: tele-

[36] See for example, Viscount Montgomery, *Memoirs*, London, 1958, Chapter 29, *passim*.
[37] *Times*, 16 March, 1962.

grams, dispatches and minutes.[38] It should be noted, however, that in this case as in others the selection of papers which is circulated to the Cabinet is made up by the Ministry concerned and inevitably subject to limitation on the obvious grounds of bulk and, exceptionally, in the interests of secrecy too.

But it is at this supreme, Cabinet level that a host of other influences and factors make themselves felt. Whereas officers of the Diplomatic Service and the Armed Forces are specialists expected and entitled to offer advice and data only about matters which are within their special competence, members of the Cabinet are, of course, leaders of their party, Members of Parliament, public figures and, above all, politicians engaged in the struggle for office and political power. They cannot and do not approach external affairs in isolation from all other matters and from all advice save that proferred by their officials. Accordingly, it cannot be assumed that major foreign policy decisions are made with exclusive reference to foreign issues or even to a broad and formal conception of national security in the international context.

[38] But Herbert Morrison once told an interviewer that he rarely read Foreign Office papers: he made do with briefs prepared by his own staff on whatever topics were up for discussion. Angelo Hüsler, *Contribution à l'étude de l'élaboration de la politique étrangère britannique (1945-56)*. Geneva, 1961, p. 30.

IV

The Domestic Environment

'The *Times* has made many Ministries' – WALTER BAGEHOT

(i)

WHILE we tend to distinguish fairly sharply between home and abroad, internal and external, foreign and native, it is evident that in affairs of state no clear line can be drawn between the two classes of affairs. The greatest single issue facing contemporary Britain – its proposed membership in the European Common Market – pertains wholly neither to the foreign nor to the domestic sphere, nor, for that matter, solely or even predominantly to the political or the economic or the military, but to all in something like equal degree. And this, of course, is merely another way of suggesting that such categories as 'foreign' and 'domestic', and 'political', 'economic' and 'military' are so narrow and exclusive of substance as to tend to be ambiguous and misleading where no attempt is made to employ them with suitably heavy reservations and qualifications.

Seen from the vantage point of the policy-maker, however, certain broad – and, of course, traditional – distinctions can be made. They are partly functions of administrative convenience: most affairs of government are related, ultimately, one to another, but if they are to be handled efficaciously they must be parcelled out amongst various teams of ministers and officials. These tend, with time, to gain special familiarity with certain loose classes of business and to develop specifically departmental techniques and procedures for habitual, if not automatic, application to individual cases as they arise. And accordingly, as we have seen, a great part of government business is the central management and coordination of such specialist teams. The theory is that at the highest level of authority – in the Cabinet – all strings are pulled together and the narrowly bureaucratic, essentially nominal, but extremely convenient distinctions between classes of affairs made to dissolve. When this does not happen to a really significant degree – which is, by all accounts, much of the time – it is in great part due to the vast inertial strength of those traditional administrative and constitutional distinctions and procedures. And these tend to be weighed down by all the natural encrustations of formed minds, private interests and personal inclinations which naturally accrue in a long-established and socially and politically prestigious bureaucracy.

But it is not only administrative convenience that tends to encourage the separate consideration of questions that appear, at least in the first instance, to be related to events beyond the legal boundaries of the state as opposed to developments within them. The first business of a government is to ensure its own survival. Except where a government is subject to subversion by a foreign power, the political survival of the group or party in power is almost exclusively dependent upon internal factors: the strength of the opposition, electoral fortunes, the cohesion of the group in power, the capacity of the leaders to dominate their own immediate followers, and so forth. All these matters evolve within the borders of the state and to that extent the distinction between domestic politics and international politics is a useful and valid one, even if not absolutely free of ambiguity.[1] Nevertheless, the form which the political struggle takes in Britain is predominantly that of a conflict over policy – its substance and its execution – and the question that arises is whether conflict over *foreign* policy plays a role of any marked significance in that struggle. For clearly if it does, then the conduct of the government in the external context will hinge to a significant extent on what is politic in the domestic.

The fact is that there can be little doubt that foreign affairs play only a very limited role in British domestic politics – these being conceived as the organized quest for formal power and the conflicts that are consequent upon it. Some of the reasons for this are inherent in the nature of international affairs and their management by governments. Other reasons, possibly the more important ones, seem traceable back to certain characteristics of British society in general and British political life in particular.

Something has already been said of the extreme complexity of international affairs, and the relative nature of any particular view, description or analysis of them.[2] It follows that a simple view of a given diplomatic issue or world development is not really possible so long as the discussion proceeds on the level of facts and their interpretation. Simplicity betokens ignorance –wilful or unwitting. (Conversely,

[1] More than one modern British Prime Minister has regarded his relations with the President of the United States as being of significance in internal politics.

[2] Cf. Chapter I.

ignorance of detail entails simplicity.) It is thus extraordinarily difficult
to make problems in foreign affairs readily comprehensible to the public at large; and any projection of an international problem into the
domestic political arena is likely to lead to distortion of its elements,
or else to its being discussed only in those normative terms which are
appropriate to, or which lend themselves to, public debate. Thus the
great contemporary problem of the military presence of the United
States in South-east Asia and the related question of Britain's alignment with the United States in that part of the world were very much
issues in British domestic politics in 1967 – notably at the Scar-
borough Labour Party Conference. The Party's left-wing took public
issue with the parliamentary leader on this matter, to their intense
annoyance and embarrassment. But in the course of its transfer to the
domestic scene this immensely complex issue on the solution of which
the political shape of South-east Asia throughout the present century
may reasonably be said to hinge was pared down to the entirely legi-
timate but nevertheless narrow question whether Britain could properly support the United States while the latter was engaged in the
bombing of North Vietnamese towns and villages. Thus the ground
was shifted from the detailed political-strategic one which only experts were really competent to debate to the ethical one in which anyone could join.

To the fact that informed and systematic discussion of foreign affairs
is a business for experts must be added the circumstances that much
diplomacy is secret and that the goals of policy may be obscure even
to the initiated, or deliberately held from the public, or so general in
content (e.g. 'the maintenance of national security') that all political
groups necessarily and willingly subscribe to them. Matters such as
these do not lend themselves to internal political debate nearly as
easily as questions of wages, or housing, or pensions, or the condition
of the railways. Moreover, every citizen knows something about economic and social questions, if only unsystematically, and almost all citizens care, and many care greatly, about them. But all the evidence
shows that this is not the case where foreign affairs are concerned:
the bulk of the population knows little about them and cares less. In
every election campaign since the Second World War it has been
questions of social and economic policy – and achievement – that
have dominated, while defence and foreign affairs have played a very
minor role, if any. The British public's interest in political affairs of
any description is in any case not particularly striking.[3] Its interest

[3] According to one study only 15% of the British public is 'very interested'
in politics; 37% are 'interested'; 33% are 'not really interested'; and 15% are

in foreign affairs is smaller still. It has been established – and it is typical – that during the long and bitter dispute over Palestine and over Britain's handling of it while it held the Mandate the only period when the large proportion of 'undecided' opinion dropped heavily and the demand for evacuation rose was when British troops came under heavy attack. And it could be concluded, in the words of a former Minister of State at the Foreign Office, that 'the [public] urge to leave Palestine ... had nothing to do with the major questions of British obligations to Jew or Arab or of *British interests in the Middle East*. It was simply an expression of disgust.[4]

The suitability of foreign affairs to the formalized disputes of internal politics are still further reduced by the fact that where opinion is divided on foreign questions the divisions tend not to be along the classic party lines. Thus whereas a partisan 'cleavage' between the major parties is readily noticeable on such topics as taxes, social services, nationalization and industrial relations, there is little or no evidence of partisanship on such topics as the recognition of East Germany, policy towards Spain, nuclear disarmament or the European Common Market.[5] And there is the further circumstance that since the Second World War leaders of both major parties have been in broad agreement on long-term major policy: the American Alliance, the independent nuclear deterrent and, with the change in Labour's position that occurred in 1966, on entry into the European Common Market as well. There has been disagreement – on the timing of the successive withdrawals from the Middle East, for example, and on the vigour with which a stated policy has been pursued. And there has been room for criticism of the tactics adopted or of the emphasis given particular facets of policy – the United States 'relationship' as opposed to the European orientation, for example. But where the broad outline of policy and the purposes underlying it have been seriously questioned, the questions have tended to come principally from within the parties – and especially from within the Labour Party – and the critical disputes have been between the leaders and their own supporters.

Some other factors militating against the injection of foreign policy issues into domestic politics and in favour of a bi-partisan approach may be mentioned. Firstly, the traditional arguments for bi-partisanship (the principle that domestic quarrels should be subordinated to

'not at all interested'. Mark Abrams, 'Social Trends and Electoral Behaviour,' *British Journal of Sociology*, 1962, p. 233.

[4] Kenneth Younger, 'Public Opinion and Foreign Policy', *British Journal of Sociology*, 1955, p. 172. (Italics added.)

[5] J. Blondel, *Voters, Parties and Leaders*, London, 1963, pp. 76–7.

the dictates of national honour, the patriotic requirement to uphold the national interest in the face of foreign opposition) are still held in respect. It can be impolitic to oppose the government in times of crisis because of the possible charges of disloyalty. Most front-rank political leaders will abstain from publicly criticizing government policy while travelling abroad. Secondly, the British system of alternative governments implies that the opposition of today is the government of tomorrow and that the government of today is the opposition of tomorrow. A new government cannot easily shrug off international obligations entered into by its predecessor and in theory formal treaty obligations cannot be shrugged off at all. On the other hand the rate of change in the structure of international affairs tends to be lower than in domestic, certainly in Britain with its parliamentary system and legal opposition. And thus the external environment – at any rate, as conceived and analysed by the Executive's experts – may remain unchanged in all but detail for years at a time. Thirdly, many party leaders in opposition will have served as ministers and almost all will have served a very long apprenticeship in active politics. Their experience of practical affairs and, in particular, their experience of political decision-making will therefore generally be very much greater than that of their followers. This in itself will serve to inhibit hasty criticism of the Government. Moreover, since Government and Opposition leaders alike will have learned about the world beyond the British Isles chiefly, if not wholly, from the same civil service instructors there is at least the basis of a common outlook. Indeed, it is only when a party has been in opposition for a very long period – as was the Labour Party between 1951 and 1964 – and the proportion of former ministers on the Opposition front bench drops below the normal that these brakes on the public pursuit of a partisan foreign policy tend to erode. And even then the expectation of office in the future prevents their fading utterly.

The net result of the relative insulation of foreign affairs from the kind of friction that other sectors of governmental activity are subjected to as a matter of course and as a consequence of – and, logically, in order to justify – the internal struggle for power in the country is greatly to enhance the freedom with which the Executive conducts these affairs.

The fact that it is rare for there to be consistent and systematic clashes between the parties on foreign affairs means that the full weight of a party's official publicity and research machinery will not normally be brought to bear on these matters. Furthermore, the public's general lack of interest in external policy tends to be taken as a datum and accepted with some complacency. Certainly, no very serious effort has been made by modern party leaders to stimulate broad public opposition to – or support for – some aspect of the national posture in international affairs, with the possible exception of the actions of the Labour Party's leaders over the Suez campaign. Gladstone's Mid-lothian Campaign would probably be judged aberrant today. On the other hand, the fact that such public discussion of foreign affairs as has any political weight takes place within the parties and is, typically, a dispute between the leadership and a section of its backbench sup-porters in Parliament or their ideological associates outside Parliament, means that when disputes arise Government leaders can employ the full weight of their political and moral authority and their discip-linary powers over their parliamentary followers to stifle all but the most vocal and rebellious spirits without having to worry very much about pressure from the Opposition at the same time. The survival of the government is in any case never seriously in doubt. No govern-ment of modern Britain has been forced to resign by an adverse parlia-mentary vote as such. It is the prestige of the government, its public image, its capacity to exert moral influence, its ability to approach new problems unfettered and unhindered by failure to deal trium-phantly with old ones that is in question. It is this that can be dam-aged by a loss of substantial parliamentary support from among its own followers. In the justly celebrated, but nevertheless unique, case of the vote of confidence on Chamberlain's conduct of the war in 1940 it was just such a loss of support from among his own followers that led to his resignation. But in less critical times, when less critical issues are at stake, such a draining away would be unlikely to occur and could be easily met with all the sanctions at the disposal of the Whip. Faced in 1966 and 1967 with increasingly frequent and vocal rebellion in the ranks over his economic policy, over Vietnam, over defence policy and over the decision to apply for entry into the Com-mon Market, Mr Harold Wilson eventually turned against the rebels. At one stage, after over sixty Labour MP's had abstained on a vote on the Defence White Paper, the Prime Minister threatened to dissolve Parliament if they did not rally round:

'The parliamentary party has its rights and so has the Government, [he told them] including the right of appeal to the country for a fresh mandate with supporters who can be counted upon to support the Government.'[6]

---

[6] *Times*, 3 March, 1967.

When two months later, despite the Prime Minister's warning, no less than eighty-seven MP's defied the whip in a division on the application to enter the EEC, seven Parliamentary Private Secretaries who were among them were summarily dismissed the following day.[7] After that Mr Wilson's hold over the Parliamentary Party was not seriously questioned until the post-devaluation crisis at the beginning of 1968 shattered the prestige of the party's leader almost beyond repair.

A rebel against foreign policy is, if anything, in a more difficult situation than a rebel against domestic policy. Partly, this is because party leaders must tread more softly where social and economic policy is concerned. Partly, it is because internal economic interests tend to be represented—and openly represented—in Parliament, while for questions in foreign policy there can be no real equivalent, there being, in principle, only one, 'national' interest. But it is also a function of the fact that the parties' ideological common denominators are in each case cast in terms of social and economic policy. Profound differences of outlook on such economic and social questions are therefore unlikely to arise within a party. In the case of foreign affairs, particularly when they have been converted into such terms of constitutional or ethical principle as will make public debate possible, there is no such impediment. And in consequense such debates often tend to cut across party lines. When this occurs the rebel renders himself doubly exposed: he cuts himself off from his own party on an issue which must be marginal to the party as such; and he remains subject to the hostility of the other side because his position on the major social and economic issues will not necessarily have been altered. Certainly, a foreign affairs issue would be the least promising issue on which to resolve to cross the floor of the House. In brief, rebellion against the party leadership is a dangerous and unprofitable venture, and doubly so when one's own leaders are in power.

'It is only when a topic arises of overwhelming importance to the country, or of which the Member can claim to have made a special study, or which closely affects his constituency, that he begins to consider his duty as a Member of Parliament in addition to his duty as a member of his party.... It would be no more impressive, and certainly less conducive to strong and steady government, if every Member on every occasion found it necessary to refer to his conscience every item of advice given by his party's acknowledged expert on the subject, since on 95 per cent of such subjects, his conscience would have nothing to say to him at all.'[8]

[7] Two of the seven PPS's were taken back into the fold in October of that year.
[8] Nigel Nicholson, *People and Parliament*, London, 1958, p. 71.

It is a source of additional strength to the Ministers that they and they alone have the 'inside story of events; the ready access to the Treasury, the Bank of England and the Foreign Office; the means of tapping and processing information that exists in the unofficial worlds of commerce and industry'[9] and, even more so, in the official world of international relations. But the effective and major sources of information – brief instances of 'personal diplomacy' apart – are the permanent officials. And their permanence is well worth stressing in this context for it is they alone who know precisely what decisions were taken in the past and how they were arrived at. New Ministers may not see the Cabinet or key departmental minutes of their predecessors, nor are they in a position to assess the validity of the advice tendered them in the light of past performance. Yet they are bound, as has been said, to honour, or at the very least bound to take into account, the undertakings of previous Governments in external relations as they are not bound to do to anything like the same extent in the realm of internal socio-economic affairs. It would be a gross exaggeration to say that the Cabinet collectively is a prisoner of its officials. But the advantage of being expertly briefed for public debate with opponents who cannot be briefed at all has its parallel and source in the dialectical advantages of the professional experts in debate with their amateur Ministers.

For all these reasons the making of foreign policy and the conduct of foreign relations by the Executive can proceed very nearly independently of those pressures and factors which do, or could, endanger the hold of the ruling party leadership over the machinery of government. There may be unpleasant moments and there are important pressures of a non-political kind[10] which are capable of deflecting them somewhat from the course originally charted and even of supplying entirely new charts by which to navigate. But by and large there is nothing in the British political system, unlike that of the United States, for example, which imposes upon a British government the need to take into serious account views and information which have not emerged from within the formal machinery established for the administration of foreign affairs and subject, ultimately, to its full control. It is not surprising, therefore, that a former Minister of State at the Foreign Office should relate that during his tenure of office he could 'not immediately recollect any occasion when I or my superiors had been greatly affected by public opinion in reaching important decisions',

[9] Peter Shore, *Entitled to Know*, London, 1966, p. 9.
[10] See section (iii) below.

while assessments of public opinion in France and the United States did affect policy, British policy.[11]

(ii)

While the ability of the Executive to ram through any policy of its choosing is hardly in doubt, any more than is its ability to conduct much of its foreign business and to take its critical decisions in secrecy, the fact remains that it does not invariably do so. The domestic political implications of a diplomatic decision may not, in the nature of things, be of the same political quality and weight as one taken in the realm of, say, fiscal policy, but British politicians are nothing if not sensitive to shades of adverse opinion. Even if Parliamentary questions and debates are no longer of great significance in the long term and are certainly not crucial in the short term, it is unpleasant for Ministers to be pricked and criticized, however thick their skins; and longtime parliamentarians, as Ministers generally are, are habituated to taking Parliament a shade more seriously than cold calculation might warrant. Accordingly, a poor performance by a Minister stating government policy to a hostile House can occasionally lead to a fresh, revised statement being made by another Minister within days.[12] And there is, of course, the classic but extreme and to all intents and purposes unique case of the public disavowal of the tentative agreement between the British and French Governments on the future of Abyssinia in 1935 because of the public furore it aroused.[13] But more important

[11] Younger, op. cit., pp. 169-70.

[12] Colonial Secretary Fred Lee created enormous embarrassment for the Government when, in October, 1966, he failed to give a clear answer to questions about policy on Gibraltar in the face of a newly instituted Spanish blockade of the colony. The Times reported (26 October) that 'Mr. Lee's performance was variously described as being blundering, inept and devious'. Later the same day 'it was made clear in Government quarters that the answer Mr. Lee should have given to [the question whether the UK would place all necessary resources at the disposal of Gibraltar should they be required] was a firm "yes" '. Two days later the Prime Minister and Foreign Secretary presided at a meeting of the Parliamentary Labour Party at which Mr. Lee explained himself. And three days after that the Foreign Secretary made a fresh statement of the policy, this time in 'a language . . . that both sides of the Commons have been impatiently waiting to hear from the Treasury bench for some time'. (Times, 1 November, 1966).

[13] The Hoare-Laval Agreement was not a 'Pact' in any formal sense and in any case if Baldwin had had stronger nerves he would doubtless have reacted differently. Perhaps the simple explanation for his conduct is to be found in his well advertised disinterest in foreign affairs and the higher priority he gave domestic considerations.

than such nervous reactions to unexpected and unusually vociferous criticism is the care with which policy thought likely to meet with heavy opposition is embarked upon. Once again, the great contemporary departure from a long established norm, the 1961 and 1967 decisions to apply for entry into the European Common Market, illustrate this perfectly. Both Mr Macmillan's government and Mr Wilson's took care to have their public enunciation of policy preceded by careful soundings of opinion – 'informed' and otherwise – and by numerous prefatory debates and discussions. The gap between the point in time when the key members of the Cabinet had made up their minds and the point when public, authoritative and irrevocable statements of policy were made was unusually long in both cases. Disagreement within the administrations, particularly within the Wilson Cabinet made this caution all the more necessary and, indeed, tended to be nourished by scepticism and opposition in the public at large.

Over and above its control of a parliamentary majority a British government has control of the major sources of precise information on its own behaviour and it can protect them with relative ease, and if not wholly, certainly substantially, by means of the Official Secrets Act, the Privy Councillor's oath, the D-notices system and the rule of the collective responsibility of the Cabinet. The decision to reveal the full background to the evolution of policy is its alone to take and the practice of modern governments is to reveal very little.

'Crises have come and crises gone, Berlin, Palestine, Korea, Indo-China, the defeat of EDC, Suez, Cyprus, the Congo, Cuba, the end of the [first round of] Common Market negotiations. The amount of information vouchsafed to the British public as to the formulation of British policy on each of these issues, and its conduct during the ensuing crises, is infinitesimal, by contrast with the detailed publication of diplomatic dispatches which would have been more or less *de rigueur* a century ago.'[14]

There are also positive means of helping to determine – again, not wholly, but substantially – what information is freely available and thereby protect the Government's public image. There is the Foreign Office system of 'trusties' among the diplomatic correspondents and the 'subtle but very powerful pressure put on journalists who cause "embarrassment" (i.e. adopt a critical attitude to the conduct of British foreign policy or draw heavily on other sources of information

[14] D. C. Watt, 'Foreign Affairs, the Public Interest and the Right to Know', *Political Quarterly*, 34, 1963, p. 124.

beyond the Foreign Office and a handful of Western embassies).[15] Parliamentary tactics can be employed, as when the Labour Government avoided yet another mass abstention in 1967 by critics of its defence policy among its own supporters by having a debate on Navy Estimates talked out before a vote could be taken.[16] The immediate purpose of such techniques for avoiding trouble and excessively critical public debate is to facilitate the conduct of public business – in this case the external relations of the United Kingdom. It is, after all, natural that those who are responsible for foreign affairs should feel that their task is intricate and difficult enough without Ministers being badgered by ill-informed critics and either pressed into making statements that can only add to their load and incidentally leave them uncomfortably exposed vis-à-vis foreign governments as incapable of establishing their moral and political authority in their own country. In these circumstances caution becomes a watchword and clear speaking a rarity.[17] Whether this kind of caution utimately pays the right kind of diplomatic dividends is another question.

In short, where the Executive is aware that its policy is likely to be opposed it may tend to be marginally more cautious, more circumspect in its choice of verbal formulae to explain its actions, chary of arousing the kind of opposition that would reflect upon its leadership as a whole or, more seriously, hamper its work in the truly sensitive and politically critical domains of social and economic policy. But broadly speaking it has little to worry about and once its collective mind is made up it can decide and implement policy with less intellectual, psychological and political impediments than in other fields of governmental activity. Certainly, it has little or nothing to fear from the head-on, explicit, organized and, above all, public attacks of those who see things differently.[18] Such susceptibility as the Executive has to influences from outside its own machinery is of a totally different order: analogous to the susceptibility of the human

---

[15] Ian Waller, 'The Press and Politicians', in Richard Rose (Ed.), *Studies in British Politics*, London, 1966, p. 178.

[16] This occurred immediately after the mass abstention alluded to on page 76.

[17] In a difficult series of exchanges in the House of Commons (20 February, 1967) on Anglo-German relations and the cost of maintaining British troops in Germany, the Foreign Secretary (Mr. George Brown) was described by the Parliamentary Correspondent of the *Times* as having 'tiptoed through the hazardous minefield of Anglo-German relations . . . like a mouse in kid gloves'.

[18] This is well illustrated by the failure of the Campaign for Nuclear Disarmament. Conservative Governments remained indifferent to it throughout their tenure and those members of the Labour Party who were sympathetic tended to drift away as soon as the prospects of office began to loom.

F

frame to the effects of climate, rather than to its vulnerability to armed attack – a susceptibility to influence that is not immediately evident, nor sharp or direct, but, on the contrary, slow, uncertain, subtle and cumulative in its effects. For what has been said above of the relative imperviousness of the Executive to direct pressure and its very limited need to accommodate itself to opinion in the field of foreign affairs, should not be taken as suggesting that the policy-making machine operates in a social vacuum. It is only that the few effective and important (if limited) influences to which it is susceptible operate in highly restricted terms and arenas.

(iii)

Central to an understanding of the modes of government in contemporary Britain is the immensely important tie-up and overlap between the structure of society and the structure of political authority and influence. It may be that, overall, the influence and ubiquity of the social élite (or, at any rate, of its more energetic and competent members) in places of authority is slowly waning. But the characteristic and in some ways most remarkable feature of British public life at the centre – the very small number of individuals actively engaged in it relative to the total population – has been unaffected by the lateral entry into positions of influence of men and women who would not have been able to do so with equal facility and in equal numbers in earlier times. And this geographical and social concentration of influence – in the sense that 'London is really very small' – seems likely to persist for many years, or at any rate for so long as two great traditions of the world of British politics suffer no serious mutation: the apathy of the general public to political affairs where its members do not feel themselves immediately and directly involved; and the secrecy which covers the most intimate and critical of the processes of government – the making of decisions. And since it is clearly in the realm of external politics that these two traditions are most pronounced it is not surprising that the interlocking world of politics, administration, industry and finance, the press, the universities, old-boy nets, clubs, and professional societies should be of particular relevance to the making of foreign policy. The question is, how does it function and what is its ultimate impact on policy?

It is extremely difficult to define the British political élite[19] and very

---

[19] For two recent, valuable and interesting studies see: W. L. Guttsman, *The British Political Elite*, London, 1965; and Mark Abrams, 'British Elite attitudes and the European Common Market', *Public Opinion Quarterly*, xxix 1965, 2.

easy to exaggerate the influence on great affairs of state of those of its members who are not formally part of the machinery of government.[20] Nor need one look for conspiracy and cabals. The essential point is a simple one. It is that many of the politicians – notably, but not exclusively those who belong to the Conservative Party – the overwhelming majority of the senior members of the Home, Foreign and Armed Services, some of the leading lights of the national press, most of the key figures in the City, the directing members of specialist institutions such as Chatham House and the Institute for Strategic Studies and many of the most influential members of the more prestigious Universities all have a great deal in common both intellectually and socially and can look both backwards to similar or even to identical origins and forwards to a not dissimilar future. And, above all, they tend to an extraordinary degree to lead physically contiguous lives. They speak a very similar language of ideas, they read the same newspapers, they belong to the same narrow range of clubs, they have been members of the same or equivalent schools, universities and regiments and are inclined to perpetuate sentimental and even institutionalized associations with them, and while they may divide sharply on concrete issues of public policy they are generally of one mind in their view of the broad condition and requirements of British society.[21]

It is also worth noting parenthetically that while the various political, administrative and professional hierarchies are not uniformly and equally represented in this world, none is so much part of it by virtue of social origins and social formation as the Diplomatic Service. Despite all the reforms and pressure for change since the end of the war, 70 per cent of all successful candidates for entry into the Foreign Service (as it then was) in the years 1952–62 were educated at public schools and 94 per cent were educated at Oxford and Cambridge.[22] Curiously, it is not only the predilections of the selectors that are reflected in these extraordinary figures, but the tendency of graduates of universities other than Oxford and Cambridge to apply for entry into the *Home* Civil Service, if at all, and to avoid the Foreign Service. Conversely, men from the top Clarendon public schools tend markedly to apply for entry into the Diplomatic Service and to avoid the Home Civil.

The effect of the common background and outlook of so many of

[20] 'History would have been somewhat different in this country if he [Wickham Steed] had remained editor of *The Times* [rather than Geoffrey Dawson]'. A. L. Rowse, *All Souls and Appeasement*, 1961, p. 6.

[21] Cf. Mark Abrams, *op. cit.*, pp. 236–46.

[22] Plowden Report, p. 86.

the key members of disparate occupations and hierarchies is to enhance their susceptibility to each other's influence on questions of detailed policy. And consequently those who participate actively and as of right in the policy-making process are very far from living in an isolated world of their own bounded by clear and specifically political or social or intellectual or economic boundaries – as is often the case in more narrowly oligarchic societies. They tend to frequent a substantially larger universe in which they meet leading members of other key careers on terms of comparative equality and mutual trust. It is only beyond this wider circle that the real barriers to social and intellectual intercourse are readily apparent.[23]

Here, then, is the public whose opinion has the most immediate and unmistakable impact on the political and administrative hierarchies. Here is to be found the pool of general ideas of an ethical, social, constitutional and political nature which consciously or unconsciously inform their work. Here is the world of unofficial contacts between members of different government departments which play so important a role in facilitating the smooth transaction of public business.[24] And it is here that attempts to influence policy by those outside the formal political and official hierarchies must be made if they are to be of real consequence. Not by public demonstrations in Downing Street and Trafalgar Square, or by marches from and to Aldermaston, but over lunch at the Reform Club or the Travellers, by means of letters to the *Times*, which has been aptly described as 'the house journal of the British élite', and in countless other miniature, latter-day agorae. The pre-war picture of sinister private gatherings at which policy was hatched (the 'Cliveden Set' and the All Souls Common

---

[23] No objective, verifiable estimate of the number of men and women who constitute Britain's 'élite' is possible. Mark Abrams (*op. cit.*) reckoned his 'active élite' to be some 10,000 strong, or about 0·02 % of the population.

[24] 'The understanding within the [upper] class oils the entire machinery of government. It may blind men to the defects of their colleagues – as the Foreign Office discovered with the defection of some of their members to Russia. . . . But the mechanics of the higher administration and executive action are eased by their being a perceptible sentiment of social unity over and above the bonds of nationality and the good will which grows between men practising the same profession.

'This is not, of course, to say that all senior civil servants or military officers think of themselves as upper class. But most men honourably aspire to the highest social status that lies within their reach. If talent drives them to the top of their profession they will imperceptibly but automatically acquire on their way up the chacteristics which enable them to meet any colleague or antagonist as a social equal'. Lord Balniel, 'The Upper Class', in Richard Rose, *op. cit.*, p. 73.

Room) was too highly coloured to be accurate, but it contained its grain of truth. It is in secure, private conversation that those directly involved in the making of policy can talk and listen without commitment and without a record. And while house parties and senior common rooms have probably long ceased to be important *loci* of influence in the special, narrow sense suggested here, some means of social and intellectual interchange to which members of the élite can have recourse in a regular, semi-formalized manner appears to be regarded, or at any rate treated, as indispensable. Indeed, the increasing tendency in recent years to systematize these exchanges, to pare away the inessential social elements and concentrate on the professional and political is very striking. Partly, this takes the form of a refurbishing or reconstitution of well established institutions. Diplomatic correspondents, Foreign Office and Defence Ministry officials appear with some frequency at certain university seminars, for example. And no doubt the pressure of parliamentary backbenchers to establish specialized committees to consider the performance of the administration not only *ex post facto* with eyes fixed chiefly on the financial aspect of affairs, but in an effort to understand and assess policy on the basis of information made available to them by the Executive, may be seen as very much part of the move away from reliance on smoking-room gossip, incomplete and random data and faith in the wisdom of the decision-makers and their aides.[25]

But the most interesting modern departure from the traditional pattern of informal consultation is the establishment of private, non-governmental institutions which set out to encourage and sponsor the study of problems which are either identical to those which preoccupy the administration or else which differ only in approach, angle of vision, time-scale or sources. Probably the most remarkable and influential of these bodies is the Institute for Strategic Studies.

The ISS is not alone in its chosen field of foreign and defence studies, but in its comprehensive approach to problems of international security it is more than any other such institution closely attuned to the age of nuclear weapons, sub-limited warfare, peace-keeping forces, new states and great politico-military blocs. And this in itself is an important source of its strength. In spirit it probably has

[25] An old-fashioned view: 'Constant, though indirect, contact with members of the civil service . . . gradually eliminates [an MP's] contempt for careful forethought, teaches him the difference between an exception and a precedent, and warns him when a fire will burn itself out and when to call the fire-brigade. He soon begins to realize that decisions of government are usually right, even though most of his attention is concentrated on the occasions when they may be wrong.' – Nigel Nicholson, *op. cit.*, p. 64. Today, MP's are more demanding.

more in common with such American institutions as the RAND Corporation and the Hudson Institute than with the Royal Institute of International Affairs (Chatham House) and the Royal United Service Institution.[26] It elects citizens of other countries both to its governing body and to its membership – unlike Chatham House which explicitly excludes aliens from its meetings and membership. However, British members constitute both the largest, if not the most important national group. Carefully restricted to those with specialist knowledge of the subjects with which the Institute concerns itself the British contingent includes senior serving[27] and retired officers of the armed forces, senior officials of the Foreign Office, Ministry of Defence, and other departments, such as the Ministry of Technology, which bear some relation to the topics with which the ISS is concerned, editors, defence and diplomatic correspondents, representatives of the armaments, aerospace and electronics industries, scientists, university specialists in international relations and strategic studies, Members of Parliament, and past and present Ministers of the Crown. Its membership, in brief, is a near perfect mix of those responsible for the making and implementation of defence and foreign policy and of those who are professionally concerned with the study and analysis of some of the most important components of policy: military affairs, diplomacy and politics, pure and applied sciences, and the science-based industries. Like other institutions of its kind, the ISS sponsors and encourages specialist studies, maintains a library and runs regular discussion meetings. There is nothing in its method which is strikingly original. Chatham House operates in much the same way and on a larger and grander scale, though it has been less selective about its members and its meetings tend to be bigger. The impact of the ISS on British public affairs has been due rather to the fact that the topics with which it has concerned itself were not being studied systematically elswhere, or not studied at all. These are topics in the general field of contemporary international relations, but their particular characteristic has been that their study rests on an integrated analysis of the economic, the social, the political, the military and the technological and that they are consequently beyond the scope of any given official in any single government department. Thus on the one hand the Institute is able to provide background material for

[26] The Royal Institute of International Affairs and the Royal United Service Institution are older, more specialized and, until recently, probably better known. For all these reasons their impact on public affairs is harder to assess.

[27] Technically, serving civil and military officers would be classed as 'Associate Members'.

officials, serving officers and some Ministers of a kind which they can obtain nowhere else and which is nevertheless crucial to the taking of policy decisions in their respective domains. And on the other hand, the Institute has provided an organized physical meeting ground for representatives of a variety of government departments, contacts between whom had tended to be limited to immediate business or unsystematic or non-existent, and non-official experts. It may be that the ISS has owed its success in these ventures to the energy with which it has proceeded. And it may be that the fact that it is an unofficial body owing nothing to government support and free of official directives has been decisive.[28] At all events it is clear that many officials, from the Minister of Defence and the Chief of the Defence Staff downwards have welcomed the opportunities presented them for such private discussions held on a fairly regular basis. Similarly, the ISS has served as a source of background information for Members of Parliament, including (and, perhaps, most notably) shadow ministers, who, being deprived of official sources in a sphere where the systematic collation of data is relatively difficult, have stood in need of just such assistance in their preparations for both Parliamentary debates and future office.

There can be no question, then, but that the ISS has been an educative force of some consequence among members of the political and official hierarchies even though that was not one of the explicit purposes for which it was originally designed. Its ultimate impact on policy is naturally much harder to assess. Nevertheless, it seems to be largely due to its initiative that serious, extended, well-informed and critical debates on certain key problems in strategic planning and, by extension, British strategic planning, have occurred in recent years, for example, on the problem (i.e. the validity) of an independent nuclear deterrent. What in previous times would have been restricted to limited, official circles and discussed primarily in departmental terms became topics of general interest, inquiry and debate, both public and private, in a manner and to a degree that could not fail to be registered by – and therefore affect – the departments. It was very apparent, for example, that in the Parliamentary debates on the Defence estimates in 1967 MP's who were critical of government policy were able to speak with a command of fact and argument which had been rare in earlier years and that contemporary Front Benches can no

[28] A recent attempt by the Foreign Office to organize such gatherings of official and unofficial experts under its own auspices does not appear to have been very successful.

longer rely on the implicit confidence of back-benchers in official wisdom and official command of the detail of such matters.

(iv)

Whether it is right to see the ISS as a formalized, systematized emanation of the British political élite is largely a matter of definition. But at the very least it represents one of a number of attempts to organize and institutionalize certain customary and well-understood processes of consultation and debate which hitherto had tended to be erratic, inexpert and random. What seems to be beyond question is that it demonstrates that there are men outside the official hierarchies who are bent on formulating their own view of public questions and that there is a growing tendency, however limited, for the officially concerned with those problems to listen to what they have to say.

This still leaves a more general and fundamental problem to be dealt with. Given the essential identity, homogeneity and significance of the élite, what attitude to the external world and what views of the manner in which Britain should perform in it do they in fact share? What are the tenets and criteria by which they tend to judge questions in foreign policy? What, in a very general way, do they take as constituting a valid foreign policy? Answers to these questions would bring us to the very springs of British policy-making, but a systematic search for them, if it were possible at all, would be well beyond the scope of this study.

At the same time there are grounds for holding that even if it is impossible fully to establish and verify the existence of such rules of behaviour, pervasive concepts, and criteria of judgment, there are phenomena which cannot be ordered and explained without positing them. This is particularly the case in the day-to-day operations of the Executive, for unless it is assumed that these are entirely random – which is implausible in so large and minutely structured a machine, and in any case unhelpful – there must be rules by which some topics are given priority over others, or by which business is conducted in one manner rather than another. Such rules or criteria may be unformulated and they may be subject to heavy and frequent modification. But they are still worth considering. Partly, this is because they are likely to be crucial links between some of the sociological characteristics of British public administration alluded to in this chapter, and partly because, as the next chapter will attempt to show, they can throw a deal of light on additional aspects of the substantive question how British foreign policy is made.

V

Practice

'It is beginning to be hinted at that we are a nation of amateurs' –

LORD ROSEBERY

(i)

FOREIGN policy, as we have seen, is made within and by the machinery of government; and within that machinery it is the central, vertical column of inter-connected authorities nominally (or constitutionally) responsible for foreign affairs – the Cabinet, the Foreign Office[1] and the Diplomatic Service – that are actually in charge of the formulation and implementation of major policy. The balance of power and authority, intellectual as well as administrative, between the principal sections of the column is liable to fluctuation according to the issues and personalities involved. But taken together their control of the system is an enduring one. Even the Treasury, for all that its influence on policy is immense, can exert its influence only indirectly – chiefly through the budget and by ensuring that issues of foreign policy are decided upon with economic factors in mind, particularly at the Cabinet level. As for the Armed and Security Services and the Ministry of Defence, they function as the handmaidens of the central hierarchy, not as systems that are coordinate with it – as is to some extent the case in Washington and Moscow. A foreign diplomat in London can be fairly sure that the Foreign Office is the right address for his *démarche* and, further, that if he applies elsewhere he is liable to be rapidly shunted back to Downing Street. But in Washington he may do better if he can contrive to avoid the State Department altogether and bring his artillery to bear elsewhere. In Moscow he has no choice but to apply to the Foreign Ministry; but he is aware that the major

---

[1] In theory, the Commonwealth Office is coordinate with the Foreign Office. In fact, while it has in its own field much of the authority that normally accrues to specialists who are unhampered by competition, the overview of external affairs is firmly in the hands of the Foreign Office. For convenience the Commonwealth Office will be disregarded in the discussion that follows.

influences on Soviet foreign policy are elsewhere – in the Party and in the defence establishment and, perhaps, although to a lesser degree, in the KGB. But these latter Russian institutions are normally inaccessible to the foreign diplomat, while the White House is not.

The British system of administration provides for a carving up of the administrative field and for the maintenance of constant inter-departmental consultation to offset the difficulties that arise because given issues can rarely, in practice, be broken down into purely military, economic, political and other components. Any attempt to do so would generally lead to distortions and misconceptions. The traditional method of coping administratively with the complexity of real-world problems is to ensure that all departmental points of view are taken into account at some stage of the process. But the corollary of this principle is that no department of state may venture outside its own parish boundaries alone and unchaperoned by others. Because 'political' in administrative terminology is the term applied to questions of purpose, intention, norms, desirability, advantage, interest, and so forth, and because the Foreign Office has a virtual, traditionally sanctioned, monopoly of the 'political' sphere of Britain's external relations (along with its monopoly of official contacts with foreign governments) its influence is very great indeed and it cannot be openly circumvented in any major business – except, of course, by its own political chiefs. So while this central column of the foreign policy-making machinery (Prime Minister-Cabinet-Foreign Secretary-Foreign Office-Diplomatic Service) operates within a political, administrative, social and intellectual system which, as we have seen, is substantially wider and more complex than itself and from which it cannot be cleanly separated either theoretically or in practice, it is upon it that a study of the processes of British policy-making must principally focus. Furthermore, even in those rare cases where major policy considerations do not originate within it, but in other departments of state or, however infrequently, outside the Executive altogether, the Prime Minister-to-Diplomatic Service hierarchy functions as the gatekeeper, determining what views and data will be permitted to impinge on policy-making. So once again, it is the role of this central column or pillar of the system that tends, at the margin, to be the decisive one. In brief, it is from the manner in which the central column of the system performs its function that British foreign policy-making derives its specific characteristics and, within the limits set by the external environment, it is its practice that very largely determines what British foreign policy will be.

The discussion of the external environment[2] has suggested that the major problems confronting Britain in the external sphere have this in common, that they confront successive governments with dilemmas that are hard to resolve except in terms of mutually incompatible courses of action. It follows that the capacity of the central policy-making hierarchy first to formulate the problems, then to consider what courses of action would be appropriate, and finally to establish criteria by which one course of action may be selected out of a number of alternatives, will chiefly govern behaviour. Ultimately, therefore, it is the mental and intellectual perspectives of the politicians and officials most concerned and most deeply involved in the process that must be understood if a coherent picture of British foreign policy-making practice is to be drawn.[3]

Only very rarely in the modern period has British peace-time foreign policy-making been dominated, let alone determined, by a single individual. In the present century[4] only two major exceptions to the rule suggest themselves: Chamberlain and the attempt to appease Hitler; Eden and the attempt to prize out Nasser. It is generally accepted that the impulsion underlying the latter case arose partly out of a fear of repeating the former. And they have much in common in other respects. Both Chamberlain and Eden, as Prime Ministers, were unquestioned and unquestionable masters of the

[2] Cf. Chapter II.

[3] A vast number of individuals function in many different roles and to greatly varying effect in this huge and complex administrative machine. Such an attempt as this to isolate the common denominators of practice can barely amount to more than a crude and imperfect scheme. What follows is therefore offered as a set of working hypotheses, the principal value of which (it is suggested) is that taken together they make a coherent and reasonably consistent view of the whole possible. Admittedly, these hypotheses cannot be fully substantiated, but at best shown to be plausible, and that by scattered evidence of unequal reliability and penetration. Other hypotheses of greater refinement and precision and based on closer knowledge of the machine than an academic observer can come by are certainly possible. It is for the individual reader to consider how far the paucity of such studies in the literature is due to the inherent intractibility of the subject and how far to the common reluctance of those best qualified to apply their minds to the problem and/or to put pen to paper.

[4] In the previous century Lord Salisbury can be said to have dominated both the policy-making and the policy-making *machinery*, including the Foreign Office. (He gave up the FO in October, 1900.) Chamberlain circumvented the machinery, rather than dominated it, but the effect, in matters of central concern, was much the same. Eden seems to have done both at various times.

Executive; both ignored and circumvented their official advisers; both relied heavily on their personal judgment, or intuition; and both failed to achieve their goals. Clearly, it would be logically improper to infer from these cases that official advisers had best be heeded and personal intuition suppressed. But not unnaturally, perhaps, and despite the *non sequitur*, many observers have done so and taken Chamberlain's and Eden's respective failures as evidence that the traditional modes are best adhered to. What are the traditional modes?

The making of foreign policy in Britain is a group activity and the effective groups are composed of both politicians and civil servants. The politicians contribute their constitutional authority as ministers of the Crown, the civil servants contribute their hardly less compelling authority as guardians of both the information that is essential to the taking of decisions and of the levers of control of the administrative machine. The politicians can give orders to the officials, but this is counter-balanced in large measure by their dependence on them. Having no access to the state papers of their predecessors they remain in some ignorance of the past even after assuming office, and their acquaintance with the present can never be great, rarely more than acquaintance with the pre-digested information served up to them: 'Few Ministers have time or inclination to read long papers. Their injunction almost invariably is: "Do try to keep it short".'[5] But the relationship admits of great variation. If they remain long enough in office, like Eden, the distinction between their amateur status and the professional status of their advisers will tend to blur or disappear. If they are of sufficient intellectual arrogance to ignore professional advice, like Chamberlain, the distinction between amateur and professional will not figure at all. Again, the more junior the minister, the smaller will be his first hand experience of public, as opposed to party, affairs and the greater his dependence on his officials. On the other hand, prime ministers, over and above their extended experience, have the advantage of being able to call upon the official advice of officials in all departments, including their own private team in the Cabinet Office. And finally, where ministers can or must concentrate for long periods on very few issues they tend to acquire that authoritative familiarity with detail that is one of the more important distinctions between amateurs and professionals. But on the whole the balance between ministers and officials is an uneven one. Generally it is the officials' responsibility for defining issues, envisaging consequences and proposing policy that is crucial.

Yet if the influence of the civil servants is, quite naturally and pro-

[5] Lord Strang, *Home and Abroad*, London, 1956, p. 16 fn.

perly, a function of their accumulated knowledge and experience, the structure of the service, and of the Foreign Office in particular, is such that, generally, the authority of a single officer is inversely related to his command of the detail of a specific question. The higher his place in the hierarchy, the more remote he must become from the details of the matters he is considering.[6] Consequently, if the machine is to function properly the senior official, no less than the minister, must be prepared to call upon and consult with the junior. More so than the minister, in fact, because ideally, at any rate, the strength of the official, however senior, is his expertise, while the strength of the minister is derived from the totally distinct world of domestic politics where purely intellectual standards as such are barely relevant.

Amenability to persuasion, an ability to compromise, and a capacity for 'seeing all sides of a question' are part of the essential equipment for success in an administrative system where no individual operates entirely on his own. Normally there can be very little room for a strong, simple – or simplifying – view of affairs unimpeded by reservations and glosses. Once again, the abnormal cases of Chamberlain and Eden – each with his sharp, uncompromising and uncompromised view of both the situation confronting him and of the action required to deal with it – serve to indicate the characteristics of the norm. It is only in wartime, when the goals of state policy tend to emerge relatively smoothly out of an apparently simple environment, that something like the coherence of such dramatically crude and straightforward policies as those pursued by Chamberlain and Eden may be said to obtain – only to lapse once more into that sophisticated treatment of irreconcilables which is the peace-time norm once the fighting has stopped.

Not surprisingly, there is very little room here for the rebellious, the maverick, or the proud. Ministers come to office after many years of apprenticeship on the back-benches and after of long training in obedience to superior authority, in compromise with equals, in reliance on their officials and in the manipulation of language as much to disguise their purposes as to enunciate them. The training of

---

[6] This is not to be taken as a smooth and absolute rule. A very senior official, say a Deputy Under-Secretary, will have served in a number of countries before assuming his present post and will retain a measure of familiarity with the issues relating to them. Nevertheless, for most purposes, this familiarity will be subject to erosion with the passage of time, as will the issues themselves. New men with fresh expertize will emerge as the nominal – and indeed, actual – authorities on the range of topics that are immediately in question, even though their seniors may, coincidentally, know more than a little about the general background.

officials in the arts of obedience and self-abnegation is deeper still. Indeed, 'if officials are stubborn or self-opinionated, public business will not be expeditiously done', writes Lord Strang; 'and the first duty of an official is to see that public business is expeditiously done, indeed that is what he exists for'. While for those who differ it is hard going.

'It is here that the effect of official life on the official's mind is most to be looked for. After years of conforming to other men's decisions and of presenting and defending other men's views, one of two things is likely to happen. To the stronger spirits, the dichotomy will in time become less and less tolerable – we do not grow patient as we grow older. In the less robust minds, the distinction will become blurred: the time will come when they will hardly have any views of their own, or, if they have, will hardly know what they are.'

What fate awaits those who are of 'robust' cast of mind Lord Strang does not make clear. But he suggests that real difficulty with them is infrequent, for

'Within the Foreign Office itself, the events of international life are seen to be very compelling, and it is rare for the Minister and his staff not to see them in much the same light.'[7]

'The first duty of an official is to see that public business is expeditiously done' and 'the events of international life are seen to be very compelling'. It is well worth pondering these dicta. They contain in encapsulated form, the heart of the matter.

(ii)

The pressure of work on those ministers and officials – particularly the senior amongst them – who are directly concerned with foreign affairs is immense. It can be gauged by the volume of reporting that flows into the Foreign Office. In the year 1962 14,500 formal ambassadorial dispatches of the traditional kind, 75,000 telegrams and a quarter of a million other pieces of correspondence flowed in. The outgoing traffic was greater still. The volume of reporting is many times greater than that of the inter-war years, and the tendency has been to employ the comparatively leisurely form of dispatches less and telegrams more.[8] Much of the correspondence is technical and routine, and some of it is no doubt trivial. But on the whole this vast com-

---

[7] *Op. cit.*, p. 303.
[8] Plowden Report, p. 7.

munication traffic is no more than a reflection of the changes in international relations that have occurred since the war and to which all
foreign ministries and foreign services have been subject: the increase
in the number of new states, the greater attention paid by governments to ostensibly non-political spheres such as those of commercial,
scientific and cultural relations; the greater number of crisis points
that must be considered simultaneously; and the generally heightened
awareness of the perils inherent in international conflict regardless of
location and initial intensity. The speed with which contemporary
political and military affairs evolve, multiplied by the speed with
which reports and instruction bearing upon them can be transmitted,
have greatly intensified the pace at which the administration of
foreign affairs and the taking of decisions must proceed. And the
diminution in the number of principal centres of world power has
much increased the probability that events in different spheres and
different parts of the globe will interact or at least relate to each other.
It is therefore essential that policy-makers grasp and cater for the
intricate connection that may obtain between widely separate developments. There is a great deal of truth in the view expressed by an official of great experience, that

'There is no more onerous job in the world than that of British Foreign
Secretary. He cannot hope to decentralize effectively because unless
he knows all that is going on, he really knows nothing.'

As for the Senior officials, they labour under

'the cumulative strain imposed by the obligation to master the details
of complicated issues, to make up one's mind quickly and to give
positive, helpful advice to the Secretary of State.[9]

In these circumstances it is clear that the requirement to ensure
that 'public business be expeditiously done' is an overwhelming one.
But this need to deal with public business expeditiously has itself a
number of important consequences.

Firstly, the men at the top no doubt do need to know 'all that is
going on'. In practice, however, this means one of two things, or perhaps both. Their knowledge of most affairs can hardly be more than
superficial. And when a particular problem begins to loom large on
their political, and therefore mental, horizon and require closer attention, other matters will have to be pushed aside – as, for example, when
the Head of the Northern Department in the Foreign Office has to
spend a great deal of his time on a fisheries dispute with Iceland,

[9] Ivone Kirkpatrick, *The Inner Circle*, London, 1959, p. 258-59.

rather than on his major responsibility, Russia. But it therefore follows that the major criterion determining which matters will take precedence cannot be that of intrinsic importance, but rather their urgency – which is another way of saying that energy and thought tend to be concentrated on the immediate, rather than on the fundamental.[10] As a corollary, decisions which in themselves may be routine, but which are capable of having unpleasant – and therefore urgent – repercussions, must equally tend to be reviewed at a high level.[11] A second corollary is that those matters which do not loom too large or too noisily on the policymakers' horizons tend to be shunted into the background of their consciousness and to be dealt with by subordinates or not at all. There can hardly be anyone of great experience and seniority left to watch well oiled and gently ticking engines for incipient faults. That no news is good news is natural enough; what is possibly more serious is that good news is no news. 'There is the circumstance', to quote Sir Ivone Kirkpatrick once more, 'that when things go well they require little attention and are seldom heard of.'[12]

This leads to a second consequence of the built-in impulsion of bureaucracies to deal with the 'in' tray before all else and to deal with it as speedily and smoothly as possible, namely the tendency to attach great value – perhaps supreme value – to stability and, in diplomatic terms, to the *status quo*. Change and routine are incompatible, as are disruption and efficiency. The bureaucrat who manipulates the machine and the political chief who relies on him for advice, information and implementation of instructions – the latter being functionally related to the former – operate empirically. Operating empirically means, among other things, operating in the light of knowledge of the environment and acquaintance with techniques for dealing with it. In practice, this in turn means knowledge of the past, knowledge of precedents. And knowledge of precedents can easily lead to an attachment for precedents.

However that may be, the method by which the ideal of bureaucratic efficiency is best attained accords easily with the traditional climate of British domestic politics where 'practical politics' and

---

[10] '. . . the increase in staffs and the volume of paper piled on the desks of the Foreign Secretary and senior officials give them little time to think, to look ahead and to make wise long-term plans. This is one of the reasons for which British policy abroad has borne the marks of hand-to-mouth improvization'. – Kirkpatrick, *op. cit.*, p. 267.

[11] Herbert Morrison told an interviewer that in his experience every arms sale abroad was examined by the Cabinet because an arms deal was always a 'tricky business'. Hüsler, *op. cit.*, p. 26.

[12] *Op. cit.*, p. 259.

specific problems and issues count for a great deal more than theoretically coherent and consistent, and therefore necessarily somewhat abstracted, views of social affairs. Where 'practical politics' dominate it is not intellectual brilliance that is sought for in the official, but the ability to manipulate the machinery of state with maximum efficacy.[13] Clearly, this ability to manipulate would be compromised by a change in the rules of the game; it is natural enough that the official who possesses it should attempt to avoid change and, indeed, resent it. It may therefore be supposed that if the major influence on foreign policy-making everywhere were essentially bureaucratic, as in Britain, international relations would be substantially more tranquil. The fact that this is not always the case goes some way to explain the difficulty bureaucratic policy-making machines commonly find in attempting to cope with those states which are governed by influences of another order – personal, pathological, intuitional, for example. The latter tend to function in a manner generally predicated on contempt for precedent, regularity and an empirical, atomized treatment of affairs, i.e. dealing with problems 'on their merits'.

A third consequence of a largely bureaucratized administration of foreign relations is the difficulty of attempting to formulate a coherent foreign policy – *a* foreign policy – in the sense, and it is a limited sense, that policies directed at particular goals or events are compatible with each other and cumulative in their effects. Keeping the desk clean, attachment to precedent and stability, dealing with matters as they arise and 'on their merits' – all have the effect of inhibiting a strong, centrally-directed and, above, centrally-conceived policy. Such a policy can only be formulated where there is the will to ride rough-shod over administrative boundaries and factual detail alike. It requires either passion or intellectual arrogance. It certainly leaves little room for the expert and the specialist. It tends to be a Procrustean operation. Respect for precedent, for constitutional norms, for lines of interdepartmental demarcation, and for the individually perceived fact – all of which are, broadly speaking, central characteristics of British administration in both the domestic and external spheres – are therefore in themselves likely to be major reasons why successive British governments have allowed themselves to be confronted for so long

---

[13] 'It will be an advantage if [a head of department in the Foreign Office] is an expert in at any rate part of the work of his department, but the prime function of a civil servant is to know how to conduct public business, and the possession of this quality is in general to be more highly prized than brilliance of intellect or originality alone'. – Strang, *op. cit.*, p. 283.

G

with the grave and seemingly irresolvable dilemmas outlined in an earlier chapter.[14]

It may also be said that it is the very excellence of the Foreign Office as a bureaucratic machine, managed by a group of individuals who, collectively, have few superiors for the energy and skill which they apply to their duties and for the competence with which they report and collate foreign affairs, that is the source of its profound influence on the making of British foreign policy. And it is the fact that its influence is exerted collectively that makes it so formidable and so lasting, reducing the contribution of successive Cabinets, let alone Foreign Secretaries, to an order of magnitude that is rarely more than marginal. What has been said of the modern business corporation is not without application to a great government department such as this.

'When power is exercised by group, not only does it pass into the organization but it passes irrevocably. If an individual has taken a decision, he can be called before another individual, who is his superior in the hierarchy, his information can be extracted and examined and his decision can then be reversed by the greater wisdom or experience of the superior. But if the decision requires the combined information of a group, it cannot be safely reversed by an individual. He will have to get the judgment of other specialists. This returns the power once more to organization.'[15]

(iii)

If coherence of action and purpose are difficult to come by and if, indeed, there is a strongly held belief that such coherence is unattainable, what then is the unifying principle, the *idée maîtresse* without which the machine would fail for lack of inner, bureaucratic logic and without which the behaviour of British Governments in the external sphere would in practice be considerably more erratic and have very much less unity of style than, in fact, it does? A possible answer is suggested by Lord Strang's proposition that 'within the Foreign Office itself, the events of international life are seen to be very compelling.'

The essence of this, the 'pragmatic' approach to events, is the custom of seeing the external environment as a complex of fundamentally discrete, imperfectly connected or entirely disconnected problems,

---

[14] Cf. Chapter II.
[15] J. K. Galbraith, Reith Lecture on 'The New Industrial State', *The Listener*, 24 November, 1966.

each one of which is best understood when viewed individually. The traditional philosophical bent which informs this approach is heavily reinforced both by the bureaucratic system which makes the Ambassadorial report a principal and, very often, the initial building block out of which policy is constructed and by the autonomy with which the central and ancillary pillars of the Whitehall system as a whole (Foreign Office, Commonwealth Office, the Treasury, Ministry of Defence, Board of Trade, etc.) formulate their departmental views. The external environment is not seen as a tangled wood through which a way must be hacked towards a defined target within or beyond it. Indeed, it could only be seen in such terms if political inspiration came clearly from the top or from a dominating personality within the machine. This, as has been suggested, is the exceptional case and the structure of Whitehall militates against it occurring with any frequency.

The consequences of the piecemeal approach to the environment and the tendency to argue from the environment to the policy, or the continual attempt to infer what policy should be from a consideration of the 'facts' or 'realities' of the 'situation' are two. Firstly, it is the external event, the act of the foreign government, for example, which tends to dominate thinking, rather than the goal or purpose which the British Government itself wishes to pursue. The former takes on a hard, fixed quality. The latter tends to fluidity. The making of foreign policy becomes a process of adjustment, rather than one of creation. The end product of the process, the final 'policy', tends to be what is judged the most profitable or the least injurious of a number of alternatives; but the terms of the problem, and the elements of the situation which determine the range of alternatives – these are largely set by others. Here, for illustration, is Anthony Eden's account of one of the early confrontations with the new Nazi government of Germany:

'The withdrawal of Germany from the Disarmament Conference [in 1933] left the British Government with several disagreeable alternatives. In law at least, they could use force against German rearmament; or they could give up an idea of a disarmament convention and let events take their course; or, finally, they could make further efforts for a disarmament convention and try to persuade Germany to return to the Conference at a price. This last, combined with some rearmament at home, was the policy chosen.'[16]

---

[16] Earl of Avon, *The Eden Memoirs; Facing the Dictators*. London, 1962, p. 47. It may be permissible, without irony, to cite Neville Chamberlain's precise formulation of the general principle underlying Eden's thinking here: 'What

In the event, the scale of British rearmament was extremely limited and attempts to 'persuade' Germany to alter course 'at a price' turned out to be thoroughly misconceived. But the essential point is that the policy decision hinged on the new 'facts' of the situation – established by resurgent Germany – rather than on goals set by Britain for herself in respect of the European situation as a whole. Of course, the harder the 'fact', the greater its seeming finality and certainty, and once it is judged a *fait accompli* its mutation into a fixed component of the diplomatic scenery is complete. The *fait accompli*, a British official of long experience has put it, is

'one kind of fact which seems to get through and indeed is warmly welcomed. . . . If postponement of decision has finally resulted in another party taking the initiative and securing some gain, so far from there being any dismay in Whitehall there are loud sighs of relief. "You see, this is a fact. We have got to accept this and operate on this basis from now on." '[17]

The internal equivalents of the external *faits accomplis* are those principles of practical diplomatic behaviour which, over the years, tend to be referred to for authority – somewhat in the manner that precedents are referred to in common law – and which are themselves beyond serious discussion. For years the rules guiding Britain's relations with the states of continental Europe and, indeed, Britain's conception of herself in the world of states, were grounded on the belief that the only possible posture was one of benevolent detachment and cleavage to a fundamentally maritime and world role. Taxed on Britain's refusal to participate in a European military organization (the EDC), while pressing France to join it, Mr Eden told an American audience in 1952 that

'This is something which we know, in our bones, we cannot do. We know that if we were to attempt it, we should relax the springs of our action in the Western democratic cause and in the Atlantic association which is the expression of that cause. For Britain's story and her interests lie far beyond the continent of Europe. Our thoughts move across the seas to the many communities in which our people play

does the hon. Member mean by foreign policy ? . . . Surely if you are to have a policy you must take the particular situations and consider what action or inaction is suitable for those particular situations.' House of Commons, *Debates*, 21 October, 1937, col. 165.

[17] George K. Young, *Masters of Indecision*, London, 1962, p. 49.

their part, in every corner of the world. These are our family ties. That is our life: without it we should be no more than some millions of people living on an island off the coast of Europe, in which nobody wants to take any particular interest.'[18]

This hardly differs at all from the celebrated principle laid down half a century and two world wars before by Sir Eyre Crowe, that

'The general character of England's foreign policy is determined by the immutable conditions of her geographical situation on the ocean flank of Europe as an island state with vast overseas colonies and dependencies, whose existence and survival as an independent community are inseparably bound up with the possession of preponderant sea power.'[19]

The principles of policy guiding Mr Eden in 1952 may well have been appropriate in 1907; they were not in 1952. Neither the first decision to apply for entry into EEC in 1961, itself a tacit admission that the position of an island state with oceanic responsibilities was untenable, nor the second application in 1967, a reinforcement of that admission, brought in their wake the really radical re-examination of the first principles that alone would have swept away the remaining contradictions. The same fixity, the same ostensibly hard and irreducible factual content that is commonly ascribed to the *fait accompli*, had come to be ascribed to this view of how it was or was not incumbent upon Britain to behave in the seemingly unchanging context of her relations with Europe.

Building policy around 'facts' and certain diplomatic rules of thumb to which something like the logical status of facts is ascribed tends to facilitate the presentation of final policy in terms of what is reasonable, practical, objective and morally neutral. Not least of its advantages in practical diplomacy is that policies which might be subject to question on social and ethical grounds, but which are nonetheless judged to be entirely in the national interest (e.g. 'non-intervention' in Spain, Munich, the forcible barring of Palestine to Jewish refugees during and after the war, the partition of India), can be presented with confidence as ineluctable necessities.

Another consequence or concomitant of the pragmatic approach is that it incorporates a 'no nonsense' view of the foreign scene: the strong and the weak are each given their due and proper weight. This is epitomized in the well attested story that the then political chiefs

[18] Lecture at Columbia University, 11 January, 1952.
[19] 1 January, 1907. Printed in *British Documents on the Origins of the War, 1914–1918*, iii, p. 402.

of the Foreign Office, Lord Halifax and Mr R. A. Butler, told the Swedish Minister in London, Mr Bjorn Prytz, on 17 June, 1940, the day France fell, that no occasion would be missed to reach a compromise peace with the Germans if reasonable conditions could be obtained and, generally, that 'commonsense and not bravado' would govern British policy.[20] Shortly afterwards the Foreign Office fell into other hands and Churchillian leadership was asserted. Churchill's policy of resisting Germany was, of course, characterized by the fact that initially, at any rate, there was more bravado than commonsense in it. The essential difference, however, was that the policy of waging war against Germany was founded on goals, not circumstances; and it was, moreover, the precision of the goals and the successful manner in which they were made to pervade and motivate the entire machinery of government that gave the policy its unity, coherence and power. Certainly, it may be questioned whether it is possible to maintain in peace the attributes and advantages of wartime policy. But in political terms the difference between war and peace is one of intensity and means of conflict, not of kind; and if, while recognizing the greater complexity of peacetime foreign policy-making, one takes what can be – and has been – achieved in wartime as the top of a scale of coherence and clarity of thought and action, one is provided with a standard by which to judge the efficacy of the machine at all times.

Finally, one returns to Lord Strang's point that 'events are compelling' and that therefore 'it is rare for the Minister and his staff not to see them in much the same light'. No doubt, as the staff are the chief purveyors of 'facts' to the Minister, this must be so. But what may be of still greater importance is that where facts and pseudo-facts – as distinct from goals and purposes – dominate thinking, serious divisions within and among the staff cannot but be infrequent and ephemeral. Facts do not lend themselves to dispute, except as the grounds on which goals may be justified – and then the usual human practice is to adduce whatever evidence is at hand and appears appropriate. Disputes about goals are quite another matter. However, where goals and purposes do not serve as the essential building blocks of policy such disputes need not take place.

All in all, then, the 'pragmatic' approach encourages the piecemeal treatment of discrete problems. Where there is disagreement it tends to be about cases, not the general line. The influence of the individual is reduced: that of the minister because he is highly dependent on his staff; that of the official because his role is so closely defined and limited to particular cases. He can rebel; but with the flow of events

[20] *Times*, 9, 10, 11, 13, 16 September, 1965.

through time new cases will emerge; and if he is dissatisfied with the treatment of the old he can look forward hopefully to the new. In sum, there are few fixed points or issues. And while attention is concentrated on tactics the strategy remains obscure.

VI

Making British Foreign Policy

'The worst kind of diplomacy is uncertain diplomacy' – GEORGE CANNING

IT was suggested at an early stage of the argument[1] that the process of policy-making may be seen as an interaction between elements of an outer world in (and on) which the policy-makers are bound to operate and the inner, mental and administrative world of the policy-makers themselves. Up to a point, therefore, and with certain reservations and qualifications which will be made clear further on, the process may be conveniently seen as one of decision-making. There is, after all, a sense in which the considered and deliberate actions taken and positions adopted by the British Government in the foreign realm are the product or resultant of a series of decisions made at various levels of the hierarchy and at various stages of the process – practical decisions to do one thing rather than another and intellectual decisions to consider one datum, argument, phenomenon or concept as being more instructive or relevant, or convincing, or significant, or useful than another. Some of the institutional, political and sociological influences acting upon the policy-makers and those who contribute immediately to the process have also been discussed. And it is these influences, in aggregate, which prevent the process from being conducted in the pure light of reason, as it were, in some sort of carefully insulated, constitutionally established and authorized political seminar – even if that were theoretically possible, which, of course, it is not. And this is not possible because in the last analysis the external environment is not amenable to the policy-makers' control except to a limited and uncertain degree.

To talk at all of the ability to control or shape the external environment in such manner or direction as will facilitate the pursuit of stated goals is, of course, to talk of that ancient and somewhat suspect attribute 'power'. A 'powerful' state is indeed that state which is able, by the manipulation of the diplomatic, economic, military or subversive instruments at its disposal, to influence the behaviour of foreign

[1] Cf. p. 43 above.

governments in a desired direction. A weak state is one which is susceptible to such influence. However, no state is all-powerful; and, contrariwise, a state which is incapable of any significant resistance to such pressure is *ipso facto* less than independent, less than politically and internationally viable. There is abundant evidence that Britain's power to influence other states is rapidly waning at the present time and there are signs that its susceptibility or vulnerability to the pressures other states may exert upon it is slightly on the increase. Accordingly, one of the possible tests by which its foreign policy-making machine may be judged is by its capacity, over an extended period, to maximize British power and minimize Britain's vulnerability in the specific senses of these terms suggested here. This brings us back to decision-making.

The discussion (particularly Chapters Two, Four and Five) has also suggested what the principal 'inputs' into the British policy-making machine are. It has also sketched (particularly in Chapters Three and Five) how the machine deals with them. The essential implication of the discussion as a whole has been that the making of foreign policy is in the nature of a flow and that policy evolves out of, and in the course of, the flow. But therein lies the key difficulty: in practice, it is difficult, perhaps impossible, to say at precisely what points along the line of flow the key decisions are taken because the more precisely the point in time or the level up or down the hierarchy is specified the greater is the implicit distortion of the account of the process as a whole.

This difficulty becomes evident as soon as an attempt is made to schematize the flow – to establish a more or less formal model in which the principal components of the process are set out in an orderly relationship to each other. We have seen that one way of doing this is to take the information channelled into the policy-making machine as the initial component. It is out of this information – out of the perceived, collated and interpreted data flowing into the machine – that policy is formed by an extremely complex process of blending with existing data and judgments, some such data and some such judgments having qualitative priority over others because they emanate from persons or institutions which for given purposes and at a given level have an overriding authority over others. In abstract terms, the key stages of the policy-making process may be said to be these:

1. REPORTING – from Embassies, High Commissions, the Foreign and
   Commonwealth Offices themselves (e.g. on discussions with

H

foreign diplomats in London), the Intelligence services, the specialist attachés overseas, etc., etc.

2. COLLATION, CONSULTATION and ASSESSMENT by the recipients of the reports (Foreign and Commonwealth Offices, Ministry of Defence, Treasury, Board of Trade, Ministry of Overseas Development, etc., etc.).

3. COORDINATION of assessments by interdepartmental consultation under the general overview of the Foreign Office.

4. FORMULATION of policy proposals (with the Foreign Office as the dominant institutional influence).

5. COORDINATION of foreign policy with government policy (and capabilities) in other spheres – e.g. the fiscal and the military.

6. DECISION – normally at Cabinet level (but not invariably in meetings of the full Cabinet) for matters of major importance.

7. INSTRUCTION of executive instruments (e.g. the Diplomatic Service) principally through Foreign and Commonwealth Secretaries, or under their authority.

8. IMPLEMENTATION by Foreign and Commonwealth Offices (in certain circumstances by Ministries of Defence or Overseas Development or other departments) and, usually in parallel, by the Embassies and High Commissions, their specialist attachés, and, possibly, the Armed and Special Services.

9. Secondary REPORTING or FEEDBACK on results or reactions abroad by the Embassies, High Commissions, etc.

10. Secondary COLLATION, CONSULTATION and ASSESSMENT.

11. Secondary COORDINATION of assessments.

12. Secondary FORMULATION.

13. Secondary COORDINATION of policy.

14. Secondary DECISION.

15. Secondary INSTRUCTION.

16. Secondary IMPLEMENTATION.

17. Tertiary REPORTING/FEEDBACK.

18. Tertiary COLLATION, CONSULTATION and ASSESSMENT – and so on, *ad infinitum*.

This flow or process may be represented diagrammatically[2] in such a way that the variation in the relative importance of each institutional component at each stage is indicated, along with the variation in the intensity of the influence of the external and domestic environments respectively – the former being obviously greatest over the embassies, for example, and the latter greatest over the political chiefs.

[2] See endpaper.

Such a model is instructive – and therefore worth setting out – so far as it goes. But its limitations must be stressed if the process is to be properly understood. In the first place, it is clear that as the specific problem or issue or proposal moves along its conveyor belt it is only one of a multitude of problems being dealt with simultaneously by the machine with greater or lesser attention. A truer picture, but one which is incapable of really helpful graphic representation, would be of hundreds, perhaps thousands of discreet, though possibly related, topics moving along at varying speeds, preoccupying varying combinations of politicians and officials – somewhat in the manner that a great number of conversations or messages can be made to pass along the cable of a sophisticated telecommunications system while being subject to mutual interference when the pressure of messages rises above the normal capacity of the system to deal with them effectively.

A second difficulty is that as the problem moves along the line of flow it tends to take on an increasingly firm outline or shape and the apparent room for change, manoeuvre, and reconsideration tends to diminish. An ambassadorial dispatch may be an original and creative work of political interpretation. By the time its elements have been digested and the glosses of the Foreign Office appended to it, it has taken on altogether harder, apparently more factual and objective, less debatable and subjective attributes. The difficulty of questioning expert interpretation and advice, of calling for new consideration and new data, tends to increase. It is not impossible to do so, but it is more difficult and, for administrative reasons, it cannot be done frequently. At each level of the hierarchy and at each stage of the process some elements of the problem will have been settled or fixed – more or less – by the lower or preceding level. At each level and stage, in other words, part of the decision-making will have been pre-empted by the preceding one. It is thus reasonable to argue that no problem is entirely subject to a single act of decision, but is, instead, subject to *processing* in a chain of interlocking and mutually independent decisions of varying authority and significance. It is therefore probably most useful to see the process as a whole as one of total or aggregate or cumulative decision-making along two reasonably distinct paths – one being lateral, i.e. in the direction of the flow outlined above, and the other vertical, i.e. up the hierarchical level of authority.

Finally, there is the inadequacy of the conveyor belt or flow metaphor itself, useful though it is in the first instance. Clearly, there is here nothing quite like a conveyor belt in the industrial usage of the term. The design of the product changes as it proceeds along the line of flow. The 'line of flow' itself is not a simple one but a complicated, jagged curve representing a succession of points of equilibrium any one of which may be a regression from the preceding one even though the total or aggregate move is forward. Nor is there any final, single 'product' at the end of the flow. Very few policy decisions are final and the flow itself cannot be said to terminate in the sense that a finished automobile comes off the production line.

Very occasionally, a great political decision is taken – one which appears to the historian, in retrospect, as an event of unusual importance because a great series of consequences can be shown to follow or lead off from it. To the analyst it might appear as something very like a point of discontinuity between the general situation obtaining before it and that obtaining after. A decision to embark on war, a decision to alter political course in some particularly significant way – such as the decisions of two successive British governments to seek membership in the European Common Market – these may fairly be rated capital decisions of this kind. In this sense, a new policy may be said, on such occasions, to have been passed through the furnace of deliberation and the resultant policy may, perhaps, be thought of as representing a new and discrete event, in fact a clear and definable product of the policy-making machine.

But apart from the rarity of such great policy decisions it is clear that in the British system of collective deliberation and responsibility, at any rate, even they tend to build up over a fairly extended period of time such that it is all too tempting, though very misleading, to term the ultimate decisions 'inevitable'. They are not inevitable, but it may still be very difficult to trace their respective origins without going very far back in time, so far back that the scope for alternative courses of action at any given stage thereafter may appear extremely – and progressively more – limited. The general point here is that the policy-maker, at any given moment in time, is confronted by a total situation, at home and abroad, which he must try to know and understand and in terms of which he must make the endless series of decisions, a few great and newsworthy, but most marginal and unknown to the general public. It is a daunting task and it is small wonder, to cite Lord Strang's words again, that 'within the Foreign Office . . . the events of international life are seen to be very compelling'. However, the greatest problem of all for the policy-maker and his official colleagues is less the handling of individual or discrete problems – discrete in the sense that they can be so defined or delineated by the machinery at his disposal because they stem, initially, from different embassies, for example, or erupt at different times – than the problem of discovering the *links* between the nominally discrete topics and handling all in a connected, systematic and integrated way.

For some countries the nature of the external environment is such as to impose its own, comparatively simple logic upon the policy-makers. For, say, Finland, Cambodia and the majority of Central American states the great, single, external factors in their national lives are, respectively, Russia, China and the United States. These overshadow all else; these, in crisis, determine; and it is in terms of their relationships with these three great powers, or their fear of, or vulnerability to pressure from them that the three small states must order their affairs. But for Britain, still a very powerful state, with great physical and human resources, with a political and military toe-hold, or more, in regions lying well beyond that of its immediate geographical environment of Northwestern Europe, affairs are not quite so simple. Britain's greater resources lead to diminished pressures, greater possibilities, and more numerous options – in a word, to an easier and more secure political existence than most members of international society enjoy. And it is precisely the variety of choices and the essentially marginal, even subtle differences between the advantages that may be expected to accrue from taking up one option rather than another that make the intellectual and imaginative demands on British policy-makers so great.

The long-established tradition of the pragmatic approach to policy-making – of dealing and judging issues 'on their merits' – can perhaps, not unfairly, be seen as the adoption of the line of least intellectual resistance in the face of all the complexities of environment and machinery discussed, if only summarily, here. It may well be a profound source of weakness where policy-making is conceived of as an essentially creative, positive effort to alter or shape the external environment, in whatever degree, to one's own advantage. On the other hand, it is probably a source of strength where policy is directed, broadly, at purely defensive ends. After all, the pragmatic approach implies caution, protection, keeping the opponent at bay and the holes in the dyke plugged. The basis of the defensive posture is keeping open as many options as possible, of maximizing the sheer number and variety of levers of influence and coping with attack or pressure from all conceivable quarters. Such a posture naturally militates against clarity of position and commitment and encourages attempts to conciliate, to play for safety, and to prefer the familiar and the controllable. For example, a clear stance on an international question which is in dispute almost invariably implies choosing between the disputants. But since such a choice narrows the options likely to be open in the future the pragmatic approach suggests that it should be avoided wherever possible. If such avoidance of choice leads, in turn, to a weakening of the network of *ad hoc*, and still more, of the formal, partnerships which are the basis of any international action by all but the most powerful states, that may yet be seen as an acceptable cost if one's fundamental goal is inaction.

Still, whatever the relative advantages and disadvantages of such an approach, as opposed to one which is more dynamic, creative and aggressive in conception, if the policy-makers are to attain even the assuredly modest ends at which it is aimed, there must be knowledge – as detailed and accurate as possible – of the opponents and allies of the moment. And indeed, there can be little doubt that it is precisely in this respect that the Foreign Office comes into its own as the king-pin of the entire foreign policy-making system, which is to say as a machine specifically (and superbly) equipped for registering, collating, analysing and defining the realities of the world outside the United Kingdom. However, it is not part of the Foreign Office's responsibilities to concern itself systematically with the realities, affairs and needs of the United Kingdom itself. This function, in so far as it is and can be performed, seems to be the collective responsibility of the home departments. But the great difficulty here is that in Britain, as elsewhere, the goals of national policy, both at home and abroad, can only be set in terms of the country's domestic needs – real or imaginary. Where these are not overwhelmingly clear, as for example, they are most obviously and crudely in time of war, the question whether they will be set at all depends in very great measure on the structure and character and operational style of the machinery of government. In time of peace, however, the handling of issues in domestic and foreign policy is not unified, it is at best coordinated. Problems in the latter class are only rarely and erratically thought out fully in terms of the former. And accordingly the Foreign Office could not easily and effectively, on its own, formulate and press for a coherent, integrated set of goals in the external sphere even if it were so minded. The dominant influence here as in other realms of British administration is still the individual, quasi-sovereign department.

All in all then, if the account given here of the manner in which British policy-making machinery operates is a faithful one, it can be seen that it is geared, essentially, to the handling of problems as they arise, rather than to the definition of goals and objectives in terms of which such problems as arise are to be dealt with. In this sense it may be regarded as passive in total approach and predicated, implicitly at any rate, on a preference for the static, the secure and the comfortable.

So long as Britain's reserves of strength were adequate, in the last analysis, to cope with challenges to her position, security and welfare this approach could not be regarded as unreasonable, even though some might think it unimaginative. But now that Britain's reserves of operational strength have dwindled and the challenges multiplied it is a fair question whether it is not itself a considerable source of weakness.

BIBLIOGRAPHICAL NOTE

The literature on this subject is still very sparse; it is also random in its coverage and uneven in its quality. Official sources are extremely limited: the Plowden Report of 1964 is not, and was not intended to be anything like the reports of Senator Jackson's US Senate Sub-Committee on National Security Staffing and Operations. One of the rare academic monographs on the subject, A. Hüsler's *Contribution à l'étude ... de la politique étrangère britannique*, was written under the impact of the Suez crisis and about half the book is fairly straightforward diplomatic history. There are solid accounts of the institutional framework, notably Lord Strang's *The Foreign Office*, now inevitably somewhat dated, and Donald Bishop's *The Administration of British Foreign Relations*. There are a number of articles and essays which throw light on important aspects of the subject – most of which have been noted in the body of text or below. There are the indispensable books of retired diplomats, some angry, some complacent. There are general reviews and analyses of the British system of government as a whole, of which foreign policy-making is, of course, only a part and sometimes a smaller part than it would at first appear to be. And finally there are the memoirs and biographies of the major participants in the post-war period: Attlee, Bevin, Morrison, Eden and, when it appears, Macmillan.

Systematic analysis of foreign policy and foreign policy-making is more common in the United States than in Britain. And since it is difficult, in practice, to proceed with a convincing analysis without specific reference to cases the applicability of most American studies to British affairs is a matter for debate. This is not to say that they are without value. On the contrary, very many are both stimulating and instructive. One that deserves special mention is Richard C. Snyder *et al.*, *Foreign Policy Decision-Making*, Glencoe, 1962. An important general study by a British scholar is J. Frankel, *The Making of Foreign Policy*, Oxford, 1963.

The Select Bibliography that follows is thus not intended to be, nor can it be, more than a list of works which, apart from being of value in themselves, are representative of the kind of printed sources that must be looked at by anyone wishing to pursue the subject further.

Beloff, Max, *New Dimensions in Foreign Policy*, London, 1961.
Bishop, Donald, G., *The Administration of British Foreign Relations*, Syracuse, 1961.
Blondel, Jean, *Voters, Parties and Leaders*, London, 1963; Baltimore, Md., 1964.
Carter, Byrum E., *The Office of Prime Minister*, London and Princeton, N.J., 1956.
Central Organization for Defence, Cmnd. 2097, London, 1963.
Chapman, Brian, *British Government Observed*, London, 1963.
Connell, John, *The Office*, London, 1958.
Cross, J. A., *Whitehall and the Commonwealth*, London and Ithaca, N.Y., 1967.
Crossman, R. H. S., Introduction: Walter Bagehot, *The English Constitution*, London, 1963.
Daalder, Hans, *Cabinet Reform in Britain, 1914–63*, Stanford, Calif., 1964.
Epstein, Leon D., *British Politics in the Suez Crisis*, London and Urbana, Ill., 1964.
Finer, S. E., Berrington, H. B. and Bartholomew, D. J., *Backbench Opinion in the House of Commons, 1955–59*, Oxford, 1961.
Hüsler, Angelo, *Contribution à l'étude de l'élaboration de la politique étrangère britannique*, Geneva, 1961.
Guttsman, W. L., *The British Political Elite*, New York, 1964; London, 1965.
Kirkpatrick, Ivone, *The Inner Circle*, London, 1959.
McDermott, Geoffrey, *Berlin: Success of a Mission*, London, 1963.
Mackintosh, J. P., *The British Cabinet*, London and Toronto, 1962.
Mallaby, George, *From My Level*, London and New York, 1965.
Nicholson, Max, *The System: The Misgovernment of Britain*, London, 1967.
Nicolson, Nigel, *People and Parliament*, London, 1958.
Report of the Committee on Representational Services Overseas (Plowden Report), Cmnd. 2276, London, 1964.
Richards, P. G., *Parliament and Foreign Affairs*, London and Toronto, 1967.
Rose, Richard, *Politics in England*, Boston, 1964; London, 1965.
—— (ed.), *Studies in British Politics*, London and New York, 1966.
Sampson, Anthony, *Anatomy of Britain Today*, London and New York, 1965.

Snyder, William P., *The Politics of British Defense Policy, 1945–62*, Columbus, Ohio, 1965.
Strang, [Lord] William, *The Foreign Office*, London and New York, 1955.
——*Home and Abroad*, London, 1956.
Young, George K., *Masters of Indecision*, London, 1962.
Watt, D. C., *Personalities and Policies*, London and Notre Dame, Ind., 1965.

INDEX

JX
1543
Z5

Vital, David
    The making of British
foreign policy

PLEASE DO NOT REMOVE
CARDS OR SLIPS FROM THIS POCKET

ERINDALE COLLEGE LIBRARY

507 02886

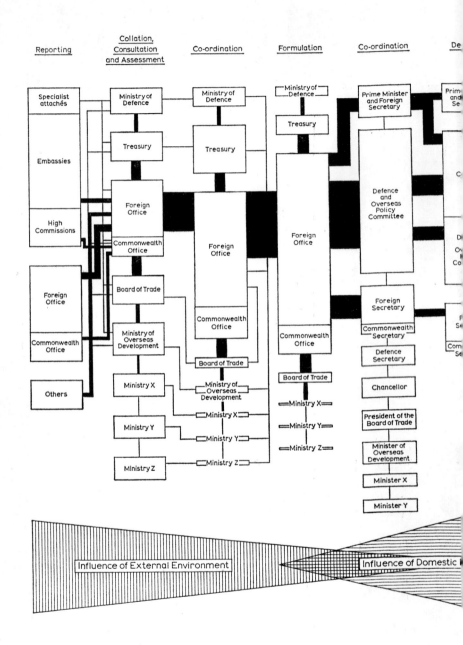

Reporting	Collation, Consultation and Assessment	Co-ordination	Formulation	Co-ordination	De

Specialist attachés — Ministry of Defence — Ministry of Defence — Ministry of Defence — Prime Minister and Foreign Secretary — Prim and Se

Embassies — Treasury — Treasury — Treasury

Foreign Office — Foreign Office — Foreign Office — Defence and Overseas Policy Committee — C

High Commissions — Commonwealth Office

Board of Trade — Foreign Office

Foreign Office — Ministry of Overseas Development — Commonwealth Office — Commonwealth Office — Foreign Secretary — F Se

Di Ov Co

Commonwealth Office — Ministry X — Board of Trade — Commonwealth Secretary — Com Se

Others — Ministry X — Ministry of Overseas Development — Board of Trade — Defence Secretary

Ministry Y — Ministry X — Ministry X — Chancellor

Ministry Y — Ministry Y — President of the Board of Trade

Ministry Z — Ministry Z — Ministry Z — Minister of Overseas Development

Minister X

Minister Y

Influence of External Environment   Influence of Domestic